NEW
WORDS

The Gospel for Today

CALVIN TAYLOR

ISBN: 0998664308
ISBN 13: 9780998664309
Library of Congress Control Number: 2017932247

All the scripture quotations contained herein are from
these two Bibles:

New Revised Standard Version Bible, copyright © 1989,
Decision of Christian Education of the National Council
of Churches of Christ in the U.S.A. Used by permission.
All rights reserved.

Holy Bible, *New International Version®, NIV®.*
Copyright © 1973, 1978,1984 by Biblica, Inc.™
Used by permission of Zondervan.
All rights reserved worldwide.

Quotes from either Bible are used interchangeably
throughout this book. The choice of which to use was
often based on which seemed easier to understand.

To you who know that
Jesus is the Son of God
and you are not.

Contents

INTRODUCTION

My path with Christianity began when I was seven years old. I did not grow up in a religious home; we were Jewish by heritage, but no one in my immediate family believed in God. I did, however, have a very loving babysitter, who happened to be Christian. My parents had been freshly divorced, which left my siblings and me unsupervised a lot, and I had an older brother who used to beat me up almost daily. One Sunday, my babysitter knew that when she left I was going to be neglected and an open target, and she somehow arranged to take me back to her house for the day. When we arrived, her relatives and lots of friends were there. It turned out that it was Easter (I didn't know at the time what Easter was). This led to one of the most powerful and vivid memories of my life.

After being there for a while, I wandered out onto her driveway and, standing there alone, I perceived a distinct, tangible feeling in the air that was totally new and fascinating to me. I was too young to have the words for it, but I knew it was love and yet more than that; it felt as if I stood in some ethereal dimension that extended forever in every direction around me. In retrospect, I know it was my first contact with Spirit, which I would spend the rest of my life seeking to understand.

Somewhere in my teens, my need for understanding led to an insatiable thirst for knowledge about Jesus. I started reading the Bible, watched various preachers on TV, and had what conversations I could with adult Christians. I became engrossed in the teachings and story of Jesus. It seemed clear to me that he was the Messiah prophesied to come in the Old Testament, and around seventeen years old I became certain this was the right spiritual path for me. I had tried a few different churches in those first years, but after college when I settled down in a permanent residence, I found a church I liked a lot, which I attended for the next six years. At some point, however, I began to sense a contradiction between my own spiritual experience and what we were being taught in church.

From the time I began with my religion, I had accepted Jesus Christ as my Lord and Savior, because I believed, as it said in the Bible, that he was the Son of God. His words, which were printed red in our Bibles, seemed to shine with truth and goodness. Yet, almost every Sunday during his sermon, our preacher would inevitably make the point that unless I accepted Jesus Christ as my Savior I would not make it into heaven, which meant I would burn in hell for all eternity.

Something about that didn't seem right to me. How did those four long books called the Gospels get reduced to this one ultimatum? Among all the words written in the red ink, there were only a few that emphasized this threat of damnation. And when Jesus did speak of judgment, that judgment was to come at the end of the world as we know it. Most of his words, however, focused on love and spiritual development.

In addition, the theme of our preacher's sermons was usually to remind us that Jesus Christ was the only way to God. But since we were all members of the church and had already accepted Jesus Christ as our Lord and Savior, I didn't understand why he needed to so constantly remind us of this point. Was the main purpose of my religion simply to teach us this only way to God?

Jesus said, "Ask and it will be given to you; seek and you will find; knock and the door will be opened to you."[1] Eventually I decided to put those words into practice and ask God directly for the answers to my questions. I also read and researched incessantly about the Bible, its history, and the meaning of its words.

It took many years of seeking and learning before I received a whole slew of answers in a most unexpected way. Alone in the car, driving home from a work-related trip, I had passed hour five of the nine-hour ride. I had been listening to the radio, perhaps daydreaming about religious questions, when a forceful voice in my head said, *Stop the music.*

I grabbed a notebook I had with me and, as though I were recording someone talking, one hand held the wheel while the other wrote down messages that were coming through. When I realized this wasn't stopping any time soon, I pulled off the road to a rest area. The words were coming so fast that I could barely get them down on paper fast enough. I knew they were not my own because I did not know any of the information being provided. I remember thinking, *Where is this coming from?*

I believe a great many of us are tired of those who claim to have received communications from a source higher than themselves. We've all had more than our share of crazy, harmful self-righteousness in this world. But we also can't let the fanatics silence the wisdom gained from true seekers.

At the time the words came to me that day, they were like gusts of fresh air and common sense, which put to rest most of the inner conflicts that had plagued me about my religion.

---

1 Matthew 7:7; Luke 11:9.

Later, the words scared me, because I believed I might be risking my salvation just by listening to them. What I was being told went against the deepest beliefs I'd held for a long time, which I'd been taught were God's commands for me to have.

I put my notebook away in a closet, where it remained for nearly a decade. Periodically those writings called out to me, but every time I tried to type them up, the same fears would rise. The fundamental beliefs and doctrines those messages threw into question traced back almost two thousand years. *Who do think you are to address such things?*

Fortunately, my relationship with God did not begin or end with the one experience in the car that day, and I know God has always been with me on my path, and was with me throughout the writing of this book. Many times when I was stuck in my ability to express something, I would pray to God for clarity and help, and it actually came.

New Words is written for anyone who can gain value from it. There is no greater ambition here than your benefit. I don't presume to know who you are or what your experience is. When I started to write this book, I struggled for countless hours to convey this material in a way that would speak to all people regardless of their religious background or beliefs and not offend anyone. In short, I was trying to play it safe, but no matter how I tried, the messages would then lose potency in my religiously correct translation. That struggle ended when I realized I didn't have to discuss anyone else's religion—only my own. All I had to do was stay true to the material as it resonated with me.

For the rest of this book, "my religion" will refer to the religion I've discussed, which I called my own for many years. Presently, my beliefs have modified to the point where

I would no longer call it that (although much at the core of my beliefs has not changed), but since this belief system is what this book is focused on, and because it will make reading much easier than to constantly qualify the reference, I will stick with "my religion."

Your religion or beliefs might be different from mine, but that doesn't matter. While I speak from my own experience, and thereby speak to you at times as if you believe in God and Jesus, these words could well benefit you too, whatever your experience is or has been. I don't state what particular denomination I came to call my own because doing so might raise preconceptions—it might let religion get in our way. And although this book searches for truth in the context of my religion, it is not a religious book.

The voice I heard in my head that day spoke as God, as a guide, as a friend, and as Spirit itself, all of which I have come to find are one and the same. Sometimes the voice was loving and gentle, sometimes funny, and sometimes expressing discontent with what has been, and continues to be, taught and done in God's name.

Religious fanaticism and denial of reason or intellect have always bothered me, yet I believe in God with all I am. Those who know God find no contradiction here (those who don't believe in God find incomprehensible contradiction here). As an avid seeker, I've learned plenty from books, teachers, scholars, lyrics, movies, plays—the taxi driver I spoke to last night—all kinds of people and sources. It just so happens that the majority of my spiritual growth has come through the words attributed to Jesus in the Bible. I revere him greatly, dearly, and profoundly. I can't help loving him. As I strove to understand his words, I was transformed by their meaning. I find, however, those same words are misappropriated and used to divide people more than any other words I know.

Whether or not this book you are about to read contains the truth is for you to decide. If you were raised in or belong to a religion similar to mine, and you feel a tension between what you were taught and your own thoughts and feelings about God, I hope these words will speak to you, and help you, as they did me.

Calvin Taylor
2015

As it is written, let us consider the lilies.

Can you know what a lily smells like if you have never smelled one? What if, from the time you were a small child, and throughout your life, without ever letting you smell one, I kept on describing to you what a lily smells like? What if I taught you all about its biological properties and how it grows from a seed to a flower? What if I taught you the mechanics of how fragrance arouses our sense of smell? What if I took you to greenhouses and let you smell hundreds of other flowers? Would you then know what a lily smells like? Imagine then you had to state what a lily smells like.

If you were raised in my religion, this is not unlike what's been expected of you concerning your understanding of God. You grew up having to believe everything you were told about God before learning for yourself whether it was true. This is faith, you were told. You've had to be able to state what you believe throughout your life without hesitation. Yet you can never know God by being told who God is, any more than you can know what a lily smells like without smelling one yourself.

This might be amusing, but God is deemed no laughing matter.

You were given reason to fear, and the reason keeps on giving today. What could make you accept without question all you are told about God except a major threat being held over you? In this case, the threat surpasses lethal—eternity in hell rather than in heaven. The concepts of heaven and hell were also passed down to you in childhood and you are still given these as the only answers to what happens when you die.

You are told who your Lord and Savior is. You are told what is true and what is false. You are told which are the words of God and which are not. You are told that to question is to display a lack of faith. You are told that if you don't believe, you will burn.

You are told that only Jesus knew what a lily smells like. But if you believe in him, and accept all his words and all you are told about him, you will surely smell a lily too—in heaven. How wonderful life will be after you are dead.

Jesus himself, however, presented you much better news: The lily is within reach for you to smell right now.

PART I

CHAPTER 1

THE BEGINNING OF THE PATH

The teachings that came through to me were like a house I came upon unexpectedly, deep in the woods. It proved impossible to simply bring you there as a reader on page one; I had to first clear a path to it by providing a context of understanding. For some, that path will be old, familiar territory, while for others it will be a new route. I have, however, interspersed some teachings along the way, where they were called for. They are quoted in the voice that spoke to me, exactly as I recorded them in my notebook. These are set apart from the main text, and in this different font.

As you begin reading this book, I hope you are relaxed, at peace, and that we can even have a little fun along the way.

You are alone right now, in your head. Whether you're

nestled in the comfort of your couch or sitting on a crowded train, no one can read your thoughts. There is no one to judge you for thinking about new ideas or rethinking old ones. There is no one to interfere with your experience here. You are free.

> Please know I am a God of love, not fear.
> Please don't believe there are any thoughts
> you could think that could condemn your soul.
> Please don't confuse discussing, questioning,
> or examining your religious beliefs with having
> a lack of faith.

Let's say you want to be able to drive a car. You take several driver education courses, you watch instructional videos, and you listen to lectures on driving. Will that make you a good driver? No. It's all of no value until the knowledge can be applied. You can never be a good driver without the *experience* of driving.

Likewise, you can read the Bible cover to cover, read all the books written on the subject of spirituality, listen to every sermon and lecture, but you can only gain spiritual knowledge when you have experienced spirituality for yourself.

"Seek and you will find."

Why are these words in the Bible? Why are they so power-ful that they are among the most quoted words over the many centuries since Jesus lived? You may have accepted Jesus Christ as your Savior, and you may have been taught that is all you need to do (and know) concerning God. But if Jesus is your Savior, doesn't that make it all the more important to pay attention to everything he said? Throughout the Gospels, he guides you to seek God; he wanted you to find answers for yourself; he wanted you to come to know God through your own experience of God, as I hope you'll see and know in your heart by the end of this book.

What you've been told about God all your life may be right. Whoever told you probably had good intentions. The question is, do you know what you've been told is right? Or have you simply reconciled yourself to believing it is, because faith is all that matters?

Either way, everything you've been told about God can help to prepare you—to inspire you—to find God yourself, if you so desire. This is not to say that any one of us is going to find a being called God appearing before us; it's more like saying we can come to know spiritual truth to which we can relate, and wisdom we can incorporate into our lives, as we grow more aware of who we are.

There are almost no easy answers to questions about God. We cannot know God completely, yet, slowly, over time, we can develop a deepening relationship with God—a Spirit that is always teaching us—which is to say a Source we can endlessly learn from.

In your search for spiritual understanding, there is no question you can ask God that God will not answer. Which are God's words? What do any particular words in the Bible mean? Who is Jesus? How can I have a happy and successful life? What does righteous mean?

The more you ask, the more answers you'll receive. You control your progress—the distance you traverse on your path as a seeker, and the speed with which you traverse it, are up to you. You can spend an hour a day seeking, or you can spend a collective hour over the whole of your life. The more you seek, the more you will find. Walking this path is your spiritual life.

To return to the example of learning to drive, let's say there are two classes on how to drive. The first class provides thorough instructions on how to drive. You devote all your time to learning the material, and you pass with top marks. However, it turns out that the teacher was quite insane and taught you everything wrong—right down to the gas pedal being on the left and the brake being the turn signal.

You then take the second class, taught by a legitimate expert on driving. However, you are still devoted to your first teacher and believe all he taught you. How can you learn anything in the second class?

Fortunately, with driving, you will quickly learn something is amiss when you step on that left gas pedal and the car doesn't go anywhere. Unfortunately, however, when it comes to spiritual matters, it seems you will have to wait until you are dead to find out if anything you've been taught is incorrect, and by then it will be too late to go back to your life and correct those mistakes.

If you had believed in a heaven belonging only to those who accepted Jesus Christ as their Savior, and you were right, you'll be spending eternity in a private Eden with your fellow believers while everyone else goes to hell. Any of your friends, family, and all other souls who didn't believe in Jesus will be burning and wailing in torment, but there will be nothing you, as a citizen of heaven, can do about it. Someone might put his arm around you and say, "No need to let the suffering of the unfaithful dampen the mood in paradise."

Or, what if your belief in the divinity of Jesus Christ was spot on, but the seeking Jesus preached about was also important, and you didn't do much of it? More than wailing and gnashing your teeth at the gates of heaven, you might want to smack your forehead in frustration.

Spiritual growth depends on accepting one simple truth: you cannot know what you do not yet know. You can pretend to know. You can believe, talk, and act as if you know. In the end, however, if you don't know, you will just have been fooling yourself. If you want answers, the first step is to be aware that you don't have them—being honest about having questions.

I was taught that if you believed in Jesus you would be saved. No seeking was required because all spiritual knowledge had already been delivered, and every question had been answered long ago.

This indoctrination began to slowly come undone as I accepted the truth: I had no personal knowledge that the answers I'd been given were true. I wanted to know, badly. I had to believe that if anyone who had ever lived had found those answers, I could find them as well. I decided to be honest and get clear on what I knew and didn't know. For example,

I knew the Bible said that Jesus gave a few blind men sight. I didn't know for sure if it really happened. I knew the Bible said that Jesus was God's only son. While I believed this, I didn't know for myself whether it was true. The more I traced my beliefs to their roots, the more I realized that I believed just what my religion had taught me to believe, since I first started listening to it. When it came down to what I knew for myself to be true, I found I knew very little. This understanding has kept me humble and always wanting to learn more, and it has taught me that no matter what we know, there is infinitely more ahead of us to learn.

If there is new knowledge to gain, how can you receive it if your mind is closed? If you're sure you have all the answers already, how can there be anything left to learn? There is a new commandment to adopt if your purpose is spiritual development: Thou shalt have an open mind.

If you are truly growing, it means you are constantly new. Think of a tree that is constantly growing new branches. With each new branch the tree is different from what it was before. Yet all the growth of the past has become a solid and unchanging foundation (whatever we learn, right or wrong, or whatever our circumstances have been). The growth is a new extension of an old familiar tree. In that growth you can correct mistakes or learn from your past. Like the tree, as you grow you retain the comforting stability of the self that still is and has always been. You do not lose yourself just because you allow new growth.

Nevertheless, having an open mind can create conflicts with religious indoctrination. I once knew a devout man named Pat. He rarely thought anything out for himself and, at forty-two, all he knew about God was what his religion taught him growing up, which got reinforced every Sunday at church.

One day I asked him, "What if you were taught that to grow spiritually you must have an open mind?"

Pat glared at me with smug self-righteousness and said, "Tell that to God." According to what he'd been taught, Pat believed that God commands only one way to salvation, and to even entertain the idea of having an open mind is to defy him.

Ironically, however, not having an open mind is what defies and denies God. The only thing most of us know about God is what our religion has told us. The only chance we have to know God personally is to let go of what we think we know. To be a traveler down the path toward God, we must surrender all pretense of knowing what we do not know.

That understanding came to me like this one day:

You can never know what lies ahead of you,
You are walking down a path you have never been
   down before,
You will come to know the path only after you have
   walked it.

It takes a brave heart to walk the path of spiritual seeking. Besides the fact that you will be moving into uncharted territory, you may have to confront a lifetime of being indoctrinated into a particular belief system and threatened by dire consequences that may come with questioning what you've been taught.

The words Jesus speaks in the Gospels, "Seek and you will find," are derived from the Old Testament: "From there you will seek the Lord your God, and you will find him if you search after him with all your heart and soul."[1] This seems to say that you should search for God and understanding. And perhaps this means both inside and outside of scripture and through your own thoughts.

Yet my religion had taught me exactly what Pat was taught: narrow is the way (God commands only one way to salvation) and being open to other sources of information outside my religion is to travel a wide path to damnation. While Jesus taught us to seek God, my religion dictated what we would find—as if the work had already been done for us. The narrow path it taught tended to be not a path of spiritual growth but of submission to and blind acceptance of a specific set of beliefs, which would get us into heaven.

The idea of the narrow way comes from when Jesus tells us to "Enter through the narrow gate; for the gate is wide and the road is easy that leads to destruction, and there are many who take it. For the gate is narrow and the road is hard that leads to life, and there are few who find it."[2]

The spiritual truth of the narrow path has gone awry. "Narrow" refers to the individuality of your own path—a path you walk alone, with discipline and perseverance, to stay true to the knowledge you have gained through experi-

---

1 Deuteronomy 4:29.
2 Matthew 7:13–14.

ence. There is only one way for *you* to go in order to arrive at your own personal relationship with Spirit. There is wisdom and direction that can apply to all, but you need to find the way forward for yourself. That said, if you believe in God, you know that you are not alone in your journey.

Even while seeking and keeping an open mind, you can still look to the Bible as your greatest source of knowledge. After all, we are talking about what Jesus meant by his instruction for you to seek, and the Bible contains all his words that we have. He said, "the pure in heart will see God."[3] What is purer than coming to God with an open and humble mind and asking him for the answers, despite having been given the answers by others?

Also, walking your own path does not conflict with going to church. The sense of community in church, of being with like-minded neighbors and a congregation with which you can feel love, with a preacher who can teach you God's words, all serve your well-being as you find your way forward. Yet, at the same time, God is available to you anywhere, and requires nothing more than your open and desirous mind to find understanding.

Jesus preached, "When you pray, go into your room, close the door and pray to your Father, who is unseen."[4] By doing this, you are in intimate communication with God. He

---

3 Matthew 5:8.
4 Matthew 6:6, abridged.

said, "When you are praying, do not heap up empty phrases as the Gentiles do; for they think that they will be heard because of their many words."[1] In other words, don't pray in a disingenuous by-the-numbers way, but rather in a genuine way.

As you seek or pray to God, it is important not to be doing all the talking, because you might miss what God is saying back to you. If you want it to be a two-way communication, part of praying requires being quiet and listening.

If you have an open mind, you will also have a wealth of resources available to you. You can tap every bit of information you receive, extract the good, and leave behind the rest. You can study the works of all the great thinkers from all the ages. How better to substantiate a proposition than with the aid of as much knowledge as you can gain?

If, on the other hand, your mind is closed, you have no way to gauge the validity of any information you receive. You will have only the very same information you are seeking to validate. It's as if someone said to you, "Tell me if this painting is the finest painting in the museum, but you can't look at any of the other paintings, and, by the way, if you don't say it's the finest painting, you will burn in hell."

It is a sad and oppressive teaching that having an open mind can cost you your salvation. You may have questions such as "Is God real?" "How did we get here?" "Was Jesus the Messiah?" Despite being given the answers to these by the Bible, how could it be considered a lack of faith to verify them for yourself—through your own inner searching, prayer, or through outside sources? Surely God would

1 Matthew 6:7.

welcome any means necessary to help you understand that his answers are true.

Think, I pray you: If you do not examine all the so-called truths about God, your soul, and how to live your life, how will you ever learn for yourself whether they are correct? How can you ascertain whether the reasoning is sound? Reason and spirituality are not mutually exclusive.

Are not truth, reason, and logic all part of God's creation? All part of God? Why would this supreme Creator imbue our universe with governing forces such as gravity, electricity, and magnetism, occurring in such constancy that precise languages of mathematics and physics allow us to evolve technologically to benefit our lives, or to land a roving probe on Mars, but then, when it comes to contemplating Him, require us to stop using our minds?

God does not ask any of us to play dumb.

You must think about what you've been taught about God. Your thinking and reasoning are as necessary for understanding spiritual matters as they are for learning how to use a computer. God, and your relationship to God, are supposed to make sense.

If you don't come to understanding on your own, it doesn't matter if what you have been taught is the truth, because you won't *know* if it is. You will only be able to accept what someone else has taught you—even if you believe that someone to be God through the words in the Bible.

New Words is not meant to wipe away what you believe. Your beliefs are yours; they are the foundation of who you are. However, perhaps it can add something to your beliefs or get you to reexamine and understand them better. All I ask is that you be open, be honest, and be yourself. Allow yourself to stay in touch with your feelings without worrying about judgment or consequences. If you believe in God, you must know God loves you unconditionally, so please believe that God will not condemn you for reading and thinking about *any* words.

There may be much in this book you agree with, but the time to really pay close attention is when you disagree or feel uncomfortable about something you read. Stop and explore the reasons behind your feelings. If you are at peace with your beliefs, mere words shouldn't rattle you. If you are bothered, it might be that there is some aspect of your beliefs you have not thought through. As a result, you might take the time to do that and become that much stronger in your beliefs, knowing why you believe what you believe. In this way, even if the words you read are wrong, they will have served you.

I have no stake in addressing the spiritual validity of any belief system, but I do think you should come to decisions of belief on your own. The only value of blind faith is to get you started. No one is rewarded for willingly abandoning reason and accepting what they are told without question. Such faith is like a flower without its roots. It may initially look beautiful, but it has no life force to sustain it, and will wither.

For a long time I believed in God, but I questioned whether that belief was right. I didn't know for sure that God existed. Sometimes "God" felt like the right word. Sometimes a great "Spirit" felt more accurate. The spiritual lessons I learned as a seeker were different than those my church had taught me. I still cannot fully comprehend what I believe in. Yet, based on my spiritual life and experience, I can now say with certainty that there is something more going on in this life than mere circumstance or reality, and within that something there is an organizing principle, love, benevolence, and guidance. I tend to refer to this something as either "God" or "Spirit" interchangeably.

I could write a personal treatise on all the astounding times Spirit has poked its way into my life—all the education I have received. I could write about spiritual perception or the internal experience of seeking and the rewards I have gained. But I don't think it's necessary to delve into what could be viewed as subjective conjectures.

I cannot look at the world around me and take it all for granted—living on the coastline made this especially true. Standing at the ocean's edge at sunset, gazing out at the mass of water rolling into shore, waves curl toward collapse as rainbows fly intermittently off their back-spray; the sinking giant sun aglow—performs its show, changing yellow, orange, red—streaking the sky in resplendent hues of pinks and purples, as pelicans soar along the coast in precision formation; the appreciation of my life and all this creation, and my utter lack of comprehension of it all, leaves me in tears and shivering in awe. This is not poetry or purple prose; it's reality.

I don't then take that incomprehension and slap the name "God" on it for an answer, but for lack of a better word, "God" acknowledges there is more to creation and consciousness than the reality we can observe. Science can go far to explain

29

the processes that govern our world and even how it came to be, but it can't explain how these processes originated. No one can state with certainty how we came to exist, we can only theorize. We can only hold beliefs about such matters. No one knows all the answers. Yet to say there is nothing more to creation and its laws than mere chance is to ignore the fundamental mystery at the heart of it all, which can easily allow us to take it for granted. Would it be safe all around to say that life itself is a wonder beyond comprehension?

Sometimes using the word "God" can be problematic. God, even among believers, can have any number of meanings. Going forward, however, I am going to be using the word God. At least for now, I ask you to refrain from jumping to conclusions about what that word means in general in this book. We are all constrained by the limits of vocabulary to convey what we mean when we talk about God.

How can we define what God means when we can't comprehend who or what God is? And what pronoun do we use in reference—"He," "She," "It"—what works?

God is real, but what does this mean? None would argue that something like a rock—something physical and solid—is real, but what about someone's feelings—sadness or love, for example. Aren't they real? What about the unseen forces that govern our reality (like gravity or even the inner workings of the atoms that comprise matter), do we call them real? Are these Godly forces? And if we are spirit (have a soul), then don't we have something in common with God? How do you say some*thing* spiritual exists? God exists in another dimension, yet some of that dimension occupies the same "space" as us and everything we know to be real. Umf!

Semantics can be a battle fought on a minefield. Therefore, it seems to me that the failure of vocabulary as it relates to spiritual matters is a fitting place to continue this conversation.

CHAPTER 2

TERMS AND USAGE

Did you ever notice how flippantly people use the word "God?" How many times a week do you hear, "Oh, my God," or, "God damn..." or, "As God is my witness..." I can't think of any other word we use so often without being aware of what we're saying. Even using the word in its proper context as in, "I pray to God every Sunday," doesn't mean there is a clear, well thought-out meaning behind it.

Equally, if not more often, we use "Jesus Christ" to express an ineffable emotion. Maybe it's a near missed collision on the highway, or someone has done something stupid, or an Olympic gymnast does a double back flip on a balance beam. I had a teacher in grade school who lightly slapped our hands for saying it and scolded, "Don't use the Lord's name in vain."

Despite such knee-jerk remarks, however, how many people do you know who say they believe in God but won't talk much about who this God is? If you ask, "What does 'God' mean to you?" you are asking someone else to explain his or her beliefs. For many people this is not easy or comfortable, unless they are among others who share their beliefs. For some, God may be too holy a subject for casual discussion (although it is often the fear of committing some offense against God that is at the root of their reluctance).

The limitations of our vocabulary are especially apparent when it comes to discussing subjects of a spiritual nature, as the same words can mean different things to different people. For example, to many, the word "spiritual" has a meaning associated with traditional religion. In my religion, spiritual meant our relationship with Jesus Christ. Others might think spiritual refers to new-age practices, while still others associate spirituality with faith in God. For me, now, spiritual means having a present and participatory experience with Spirit: my *active* relationship with what we have called God.

In my church, the qualities of God were not open to mortal examination. We were told to hold beliefs without thinking them through because God's words were to be accepted even if they were not understood. The less you questioned anything, and the more you accepted everything the church taught, the more religious you were considered to be. (I've observed this to be the case in other religions as well, which shows that it is a common human tendency to abide by the rules or beliefs of whatever religious institution we were indoctrinated into.)

I don't believe we need to slap each other's hands for "using the Lord's name in vain," but I do think we ought to be aware when we're using "God" and "Jesus" in a loose manner. If we don't, we are operating with the same lack of awareness that allows us to espouse beliefs we haven't thought through for ourselves.

The Word God

"God" is just a word. Can we humbly accept this truth? To whom or what this word refers to is another matter. Some say God is a name for the Supreme Being, or Creator of our world and us. Some say God is a word that refers to the consciousness of Spirit. Some say God is the Father of Jesus. Some say God is nonsense. Even among people with the same general beliefs, such as God is the Father of Jesus, there are innumerable variations on the specifics of what that means or how they define God.

If we are to arrive at a working definition of God, we first have to determine what we can agree on concerning God. How can we grow in understanding without first grounding ourselves in what we know?

What do we know about God? It takes humility and honesty to answer that question. Sometimes it means admitting what we don't know. Those of us who believe in God may have different beliefs about who or what God is, but no one among us understands God very well. At best, we have tiny smatterings of knowledge and varying degrees of whatever relationship to God our little minds can handle. This is all relative, of course. A spiritual master will certainly know God a lot better than the average person. Yet a master would probably be the first to tell you he or she doesn't come close to comprehending God. We can comprehend God as soon as we can lasso infinity.

God is the name you have given me. Remember God is a word and don't confuse that with who I am. Say the word God to yourself, then observe

what that means to you. You have a definition
based on all the data you have gathered about
God throughout your life. It's good to have a
word that lets you refer to me, but do not let the
finite bounds of a word mislead you from the
truth of my infinite nature. Once I am labeled a
being—even a supreme being—a definition is
created. This can then tempt you to think that
because you do not see me in front of you, I am
therefore somewhere else far away from you.

How often do you stop and think about who or what God
is—this God that you so naturally say you believe in? Do you
think, *No one can understand God, so why bother trying to
figure God out?*

In the Old Testament, Moses asks God his name and God
responds "I am who I am,"[1] a phrase that has served to keep
alive the mystery and incomprehensibility of God.

Today, religious Jews will write G-d rather than spell out
the name of the deity. This continues an ages'-old tradition
that forbids the names used for God to be written on a doc-
ument that could possibly be destroyed, but it also maintains
a level of respect and reverence, which keeps the word from
being taken lightly or its meaning oversimplified.

If we are to evolve spiritually, we cannot be afraid to
admit that God is just a word. We cannot allow the nature of
the principals (God, Spirit, Christ, et al.) to be limited by our
vocabulary, which is in turn limited by our present under-

---

1 Exodus 3:14.

standings. It doesn't make sense to attribute irreverence to any honest and open conversation about the nature of God, when we don't understand who or what we are talking about in the first place.

The Path Forward

Maybe, working backwards, we can arrive at an understanding of what God *is* by first agreeing on what God *is not*. Can we agree that God is not an old man with a long, flowing, gray beard, sitting on a throne in heaven? I believe most of us can agree on this.

The Bible states that we were created in God's image. This, like much in the Bible, has been taken literally in many of our religions. Therefore, literal believers wouldn't subscribe to the notion that God is Spirit with no form. God's image has always been defined by our attempt to conceptualize him. Would it be any less correct, then, to say we made God in our image?

It's hard to imagine if God created this planet, all life on it, and perhaps all the universe and beyond, he is actually confined to the form of a man, or any corporeal being. If there is an afterlife, however, and if, in that afterlife, there is any interaction with a supreme being (or, perhaps, lesser-emissary-supreme beings), it makes sense to me that they would assume human form, since this is the form most familiar to us. Perhaps the literal image of the strong, old, Zeus-like God would then be an accommodation on the part of the Supreme Being for what our limited minds are able to comprehend, making his image a human old man, after all. Or maybe he just began that way a trillion years ago.

In the end, no one can be sure of the form of God. Can we admit that much? Ultimately, it is just another mystery.

What else can we agree God is not?
God is not a He, She, or It.

God is somehow all of these and none of these. We are off the pronoun chart when we refer to God, which is yet another way of showing how inadequate our vocabulary is for describing God.

He

For the bulk of history, God has been accepted as the Supreme Patriarch, the Father Creator of Humanity, Infinite Mind, and, in my religion, the Father of Jesus. We have an easy time associating masculine attributes with this God: discipline, strength, and power. He has been deemed the Authority, Judge, Ruler—the Supreme Administrator of all life on earth and in heaven. He loves us completely but is strict—we must obey his laws, commands, and his every word. He forces us to learn lessons for ourselves, won't pick us up when we fall, is there to guide, teach, and illuminate the way but will never do for us what we must do for ourselves. He is father to us, as we are fathers to our children.

She

God is boundless love: unconditionally loving, nurturing, maternal, helping us again and again, always forgiving, and never turning away from us. Sometimes God is the only one who can, and does, help us up when we fall. We can alienate every human being in our lives but never God. She is mother to us, as we are mothers to our children.

The Supreme Matriarchal nature of God was addressed in my religion in and as the Holy Mother—the mother of Jesus—who is the embodiment of maternal femininity in humanity. The mother Mary is not just a religious figure of history, but an eternal feminine spiritual essence, with all the characteristics of the quintessential loving mother.

If both male and female come from God, then doesn't it make sense that God is both of these? We know masculine and feminine energies are not exclusive to the actual gender of the human being. We know feminine energy can be prevalent in a man, and masculine energy prevalent in a woman. For most of us, one is more dominant than the other. Both masculine and feminine energies are present in everyone. This reflects our likeness to God.

It

Then, there is a third aspect of God that is no gender at all. This has often been called "the universe." Some people say, "The universe brought these two together," or, "The universe has a way of working things out." Bringing the term into more intimate spiritual use, it has been called an energy field, a force, or universal Spirit. In my religion, this has been called the Holy Spirit.

I like to think of the Holy Spirit as God's medium—the substance of God, so to speak. Since it shares God's nature, it has the characteristics of the Father and Mother (it seems to guide, teach, and love us). It can be called upon for assistance in our daily or spiritual lives: How can I be happier, healthier, wiser, more balanced, successful; how can I foster better relationships with people in my life; how can I have God more present in my life or understand him and his words better?

But it also simply exists objectively, so to speak, in that it only responds to how it is acted upon by us; it is a force of Godly nature. This force has its own physics (of a sort) and laws. You can put it to work in your life. Maybe you've noticed that depending on where you direct your energy you seem to receive dividends in that area. For example, you put your heart, mind, and drive into starting a new business or project, and somehow the right people seem to cross your path. Or, when you've declared the intention to seek knowledge (spiritual or otherwise), the right book ends up in your hands at just the right time. Or, you've been injured, and the doctor has told you it would take months to heal, or maybe that you'd never be the same, but by sheer determination you manage to defy that diagnosis.

There is much more to the truth of God than the being described and defined by monotheistic traditions. All over the world are examples of the variety of spirituality and diverse forces at play—people who have accessed the power of It. Thousands of people (myself included) have walked across red-hot burning embers with no harm. You can watch online videos of parades where multiple participants have long rods pierced through their cheeks with no blood coming out. You can watch documentaries about people who lie on a bed of nails without injury, or others who hold their breaths for inhuman amounts of time, or who endure other mind-boggling feats of physicality or endurance. I have twice in my life spoken to psychics who were complete strangers but knew intimate details about me and my thoughts that they had no way of knowing (and a few others who were frauds).

He, She, and It are all aspects of the nature of God. Yet God is more than all of these. Who knows what other aspects of God lie beyond our comprehension? We cannot know what we don't know. We are limited by our perception. Consider how we see a certain spectrum of light, yet we know there is more light that we don't see, such as infrared light. He, She, and It might be just three stars in the vast galaxy that is God.

Impartiality

Perhaps we can also state some basic characteristics of God as pertains to people. Here is what I believe. See if you agree:

GOD IS NOT ANY PARTICULAR RACE OR COLOR, OR PARTIAL TO ANY ONE OF THEM. God is every one of us and none of us. It makes sense, according to our vocabulary, that we are all God's children. How can you believe in God as Creator of all and then turn around and believe that any particular group of people is less loved than another? God loves everyone equally.

GOD IS NOT PARTIAL TO EITHER SEX. Although the Bible tends to favor men, sometimes to the point of misogyny, I believe we can finally be brave enough to put primitive ideas in their place and move on. God loves women and men equally.

GOD IS NOT PARTIAL TO ANY PARTICULAR BELIEF SYSTEM. No matter what names we want to call God, no matter how our beliefs differ, whether we believe nothing, or believe in something other than God—we are all the same human species. God loves us for who we are—not for what we believe.

GOD IS NOT PARTIAL TO ANY COUNTRY. Countries are simply different locations on the same earth, where the same one species of humans live. It is nonsensical to think that God would love any one country more than another.

GOD DOES NOT PHYSICALLY INTERVENE IN THIS WORLD. Whether it's any ordinary person through meditation, the leader of a congregation, a monk, or a prophet, I believe there have been and are many people who seek and indeed communicate with God, and who, based on those communications, proceed to enact change in the world. So, in this way, God does influence the world. I also believe there is a providential design unfolding. We experience inexplicable "coincidences" in our lives that guide and draw us toward God by way of curiosity and fascination. Wouldn't you agree, however, that the hand of God does not reach down from the heavens and smite evildoers where they stand? Nor does God seem to physically protect innocent people from harm, or bring food and medicine to suffering children. And history demonstrates that God will not prevent a genocidal lunatic from rising to lead a world power, or prevent any nation from committing genocide against another.

Let's review and see if we can agree on these aspects of what God is not:

- God is not an old man sitting on a throne in heaven.
- God is not a He, She, or It.
- God is not any one race or color, and is not partial to any.

- God is not partial to either sex.
- God is not partial to any particular country.
- God does not physically intervene in this world.

By contrast, let's view those same qualities in terms of what God *is* and see if we can agree on some characteristics:

- God is with us always.
- God loves every person on earth equally:
  - God loves both sexes.
  - God loves all races—every color, shape, and size.
  - God loves all nations.
  - God loves all people unconditionally regardless of what they believe (or do not believe).
  - God loves irrespective of sexual preference.[1]
- God is Love.

God has additional qualities that are a bit more complicated, but that I believe we can probably agree on.

God is all good things: people loving one another, hugging, sharing, giving. God is delight, happiness, warmth, the beauty of creation—the sunrise, sunset, oceans, mountains, green lands. God is the eternally benevolent Creator.

But if God created everything, God is also cold, darkness,

---

1 I know that listing sexual preference is not something all believers in God are ready to agree on, but the notion that God hates or condemns gay people seems too spiritually ignorant to leave off the list. God loves everyone.

misery, suffering, earthquakes, tsunamis, tornadoes, hurricanes, death. God is eternally indifferent.

God is the cutest Bambi deer balancing on his young new legs to sip from the pristine brook.

God is the lion ripping Bambi to pieces for food.

God is the beauty of all nature; God is the savagery of nature.

God designed all; God gave us free will.

God loves us; God allows terrible harm to come to us.

Do these few qualities of God seem basic enough that we can agree on them? The God that *New Words* refers to when using the word "God" is derived from these basic characteristics, but, ultimately, God is beyond description. It is, therefore, important to remember that God is God, and we are only human. As humans, we would be wise to remember that "God" is just a word.

Jesus

There is no ambiguity in the name Jesus. Whether you believe he was God on earth or just a man, everyone can agree that the name refers to Jesus Christ in the Bible. Even those who believe Jesus was a fictional character and the New Testament a work of fiction, concede that Jesus is the name of the main character. Jesus, however, is also a name whose use it is easy to take for granted without examination.

The historical influence of Jesus is irrefutable. Leaving aside the issue of divinity for a moment, the calendar governing most of the world begins with the year of his birth.

For many of us, the grandest, most loving holiday of the year celebrates his birthday. Nearly a third of the planet's population believes him to be the most spiritually important figure who ever lived, and even non-Christians and those who don't believe in God would probably have to concede that he was one of the most influential people in the history of Western culture. Yet, the one we call Jesus never in his life on earth heard himself called by that name.

We have no way of being certain what Jesus' contemporaries called him. But the name Jesus can be traced back to *Yeshua,* an Aramaic[1] nickname for the Hebrew name *Yehoshua* (just as we might give a Daniel the nickname Dan). *Yeshua,* in English, is the biblical name Joshua. The New Testament, however, was originally written in Greek. Because Greek had no letter equivalents for some of the Hebrew characters, and because of other grammatical translation problems, *Yeshua* was transliterated into *Iesous,* which is the name used for Joshua in the Greek Old Testament.

To transliterate means to change the sounds from one language into their closest equivalents in another (for example, the Spanish mañana would transliterate into English *manyana).* So, for *Yeshua,* the *Ye* sound became the *Ie* sound ("ee"), the *sh* sound became *s* sound ("ss"), and the *ua* sound became *ou* sound ("oo"). The letter S at the end of *Iesous* was added to adhere to Greek rules of grammar, which left us with our English sounding *eesoos.*

The pronounced letter J, however, did not exist in the English language until the thirteenth century, and it took a few centuries more to become established—especially in written

---

1 The language Jesus and his people spoke.

English. In the original 1611 edition of the King James Bible, Jesus reads as *Iesus* (based on the Latin version of *Iesous*).[1] The letter J eventually entered common English usage as a way to give names that began with Y or I a more distinct sound, and so, in the 1629 edition, we see the first reference to "Jesus."

Put simply: Jesus is an English version of the Greek name *Iesous*, which is the Greek version of the Aramaic name *Yeshua*.

As with the name God, it seems wise to remember that, aside from the meaning we attribute to it, Jesus is just a name and we should not let these matters be swept under the rug of piety. Regardless, Jesus is the name we've settled on, and so it is. Going forward, when I use the name Jesus, I am referring to the Messiah of my religion—the Son of God; the one who spoke the words that are printed in red in the Bible of my religion.

As we were taught in my church, accepting the words Jesus spoke and the events of his life as truth were issues of faith. "Did Jesus say this, did he say that, did Pilot wash his hands, did the Pharisees consider Jesus a threat, did he walk on water, did he raise the dead?" Of course, we were given the answers as they are in the Bible, but having to define those answers as truths left me confused. How can anyone call that

---

1 The King James Bible was one of the earliest English translations of the Bible and soon became the popular Bible used by Protestants in England and America.

which can never be verified, the truth? As far as I could see, each of us was being asked to gloss over this little problem by accepting the answers through faith.

According to many dictionaries:

truth: the quality or state of being true
(**true**: being in accordance with fact or reality)

Based on that definition, any particular sentence Jesus said, as written in the Bible, can be correctly called the truth if, in fact, the meaning of those words is true. That Jesus actually said the words *cannot* be called the truth, because we have no way of verifying that. There is no attack on faith here. There is no denial of Jesus or God.

The truth is, we have words that were supposedly spoken by Jesus, written down decades after he died, and which supposedly were passed down with precise accuracy through all those years. We have to then rely on those words having survived through those early centuries, and having been translated through multiple languages fraught with semantic differences, nuances, and in many instances no specific translation, in order to arrive at a set of words we have no problem regarding as the absolute truth not only of what Jesus said but also the events of his life.

Many of us can easily accept this miracle—this defiance of the astronomical odds that there is not one single error—because, we say, God saw to it. God told the writers of the Gospels what Jesus said. God made sure everything was accurate. In fact, we say, God wrote the Bible.

We have to be brave enough to separate belief from truth. We can believe it is the truth that Jesus said what is attributed to him in the Bible. But what we believe to be the truth is, of course, not necessarily the truth. I believe it is the truth that Jesus said, "Ask and it will be given to you." But in truth not one of us knows for a fact that Jesus said any of these words. We can all believe that our faith has the ability to move mountains—juggle planets even—but we cannot invent truth. The truth is: we can have faith that God wrote the Bible. The truth is: we can only have faith. The truth is: we do not *know* God wrote the Bible.

I am not saying God did not write the Bible. I am not saying that Jesus did not speak all the words attributed to him in the Bible. I have never said whether or not I believe every single word in the Bible is the word of God. All I did was to differentiate the concept of belief from truth, because it's easy to blur religious belief with historical fact and accept the Bible as absolute historical truth.

That said, when I speak about the words of Jesus, or the events of his life, I am not going to use words like *allegedly, supposedly, purportedly,* and so on. For example, "Jesus allegedly spoke the words _____." Although such caveats could well be applied to what was actually said and done two thousand years ago, when I refer to the words spoken by Jesus and the events of his life, please understand that I am referring to the words written in the Bible.

Also, it has been a nagging challenge for me to determine whether or not to capitalize the pronouns *he, him,* or *his* when writing about Jesus. While many people who believe only in the sheer divinity of Jesus (meaning, even though he lived as a man he was not actually a human being like the rest of us; he was God in the flesh) will find it offensive to not use the capital letter H every time, using it could well be equally offensive to those who don't believe in his divinity. The same challenge holds true for using the lowercase *him* as a pronoun for God. Even the simple matter of whether or not to use a capital letter can become an issue of faith. Using *him* to refer to God also bothers me in its limiting God to a masculine understanding, which we've discussed in this chapter. But this pronoun issue is not a battle I choose to pick at this time.

To keep it simple, I use the lowercase letter h every time when referring to either God or Jesus. Truthfully, I don't believe God or Jesus would feel slighted if ever the usage was incorrect. I think both are above caring about our use of capitalization.

Spirit, Soul

There are a few terms used throughout this text whose meaning you probably intuitively know already. However, for sake of clarity, I will briefly explain how I understand and will use these terms. In order to share an understanding of the words "spirit" and "soul," we first have to have that working agreement on what "God" means. If you don't believe in God, the words spirit and soul might well be meaningless to you.

"Spirit" (capital S) is the word I use as a synonym for Holy Spirit. While occasionally I will use the term Holy Spirit, I usually prefer Spirit, because the word "Holy" can sometimes make it seem like something sacred and beyond us, rather than something tangible and here for us to interact with. The word "spiritual" will mean of or pertaining to Spirit.

One's "spirit" (lowercase s) will mean an individuation of that Spirit—an individual life force inside a body for a time.

To refer to this individual spirit, I often use the word "soul." Whenever I refer to understanding something from the "level of soul," it means understanding from that deepest place within you (as opposed to, say, understanding it in just your conscious mind).

The Old and New Testament

The last terms I want to address are the Old Testament and the New Testament. Many Christians would feel slighted were I to say "the Christian Bible," when referring to the New Testament, or the "Jewish Bible," when referring to the Old Testament. The Jewish religion, on the other hand, recognizes only those books included in the Old Testament. In fact, there could be no "new" testament without an "old" testament. One text is clearly built upon the other. It seems odd that we acknowledge the authority of the Jewish scripture, then turn around and identify it—retitle it as the Old Testament—merely as relative to the Christian New Testament.

Too often in modern common understanding the New Testament is viewed as an evolved or updated theology—a new way to understand God that supersedes the old. The word "testament," is another word for "covenant," which means agreement. The New Testament is in essence a new statement of agreement between God and people (that is, salvation offered through Jesus Christ).

Jesus, however, certainly did not understand Jewish scripture as something to be disregarded. He never refers to an Old Testament, or even an old way of looking at things. In fact, Jesus says, "For truly I tell you, until heaven and earth pass away, not one letter, not one stroke of a letter, will pass from the law until all is accomplished" (Matthew 5:18).[1]

There is no way to reference these books in a way that maintains their respective religious integrities and also is universally perceived as correct. It would, however, be too distracting and confusing to use names other than those by which they are generally known. Because of this, I will be referring to them as the Old Testament and the New Testament.

The difficulties involved in arriving at universally acceptable terms relating to God should provide some insight into how little we actually know about God, which is comparable to the relatively few stars we can see in the night sky. When gazing toward an understanding of what we don't know about God, we are charting that infinitely vaster space we cannot see: the unknown.

---

1 "The law" is a biblical term for the Torah (the first five books of Moses in the Old Testament).

CHAPTER 3

THE UNKNOWN

Shortly after the beginning, man created religion. He needed to somehow explain how life came to be and the forces that kept it going. Since the earliest civilizations, people believed in some idea of gods, or supreme beings, who created and watched over us, and with that belief came the need for a way to govern the relationship between those beings and us, their people.

In the same region where Christianity started, for well over three thousand years before Jesus was born, the Egyptian dynasties reigned over a religious civilization that believed various gods governed every facet of life, as well as the afterlife. People worshipped, prayed, and sacrificed to the gods for things like favorable weather for a good harvest, the well-being of their families, prosperity, curing the sick, childbirth, love, happiness, guidance through death, and the continuation of the soul in eternity—many of the same things people pray for today.

Following the Egyptians, about eight hundred years

before the time of Jesus, just across the Mediterranean Sea to the north, the ancient Greek civilization was flourishing. The Greeks, too, were polytheistic (worshipped multiple gods; for various purposes) and practiced rituals involving offerings and animal sacrifice. Eventually the great Roman Empire conquered the entire region encompassing the Egyptians and the Greeks and assimilated many of their customs and religions.

While polytheism is no longer practiced much in the West, we have a lot else for which to thank those ancient cultures. The Egyptians had a structured civilization ruled by law and order; they invented an alphabet and writing system, a system of mathematics and medicine, irrigation systems, sophisticated architecture (the great pyramids), art, literature, astronomy, papyrus (an early form of paper), glass, and more. From the Greco-Roman era we received the concept of democracy and legislative structure, the basis of the alphabet we use today, literature, philosophy, advanced architecture, painting, sculpture, theater, the calendar upon which ours is based, science and medicine, the library, mathematics, the aqueduct (a system that brought water into highly populated areas, as well as a sewer system to get waste out), the newspaper—and on and on it goes.

Today in the Western world, we look down on the polytheistic religions of the past. Despite their advanced civilizations and all they've contributed to us, we still believe that, in terms of their religions, the ancients got it wrong.

According to my Judeo-Christian lineage, more than three thousand years ago today, in the land east of Egypt, Judaism arose as the first major monotheistic religion. It centered on the worship of one God and living according to God's laws.

Jesus grew up in this heritage and preached adherence to those laws, as well as his own new teachings founded upon them. After he died, a new religion began to form based on Jesus' life, teachings, death, and the belief in his resurrection. Christianity emerged and, over time, branched like a wild vine into a variety of forms.

Those people who lived a few thousand years ago were us. We only have the advantage of being in the modern position due to the progress that each generation of our ancestors made.

If you had lived in Rome two thousand years ago, chances are you would have held the same polytheistic beliefs as the rest of your people. You would have believed as you were raised to believe and what your culture dictated were the right beliefs to have. Conversely, if you transplanted a Roman citizen into today's world as a baby, he too would likely grow up to hold the beliefs that were instilled in him in his youth.

Time laughs at those who believe they are as advanced as it gets. If the human race survives another thousand years, perhaps people will look at us, in these so-called modern times, as no less naïve and misguided than we consider our ancestors to have been—or maybe even more so, as technology seems to evolve exponentially. They will see that we were still plagued with fear when it came to God, and most fearful of what happens to us when we die.

My religion, nearly every Sunday, perpetuated the fear of not holding the right beliefs and the ramifications not holding those beliefs would have in the afterlife. Perhaps future students will learn this about us and feel the same way we do when we read that the elite of ancient Egypt placed jewelry, provisions, and scrolls in the tombs of their dead in order to assist them in the afterlife. Why are we so certain we're the ones who finally have the right answers?

Be it the polytheism of the Egyptians, Greeks, or Romans, or the monotheistic views widely held today, our religious beliefs have always been designed to answer fundamental questions about our existence. If you look closely though, God is not actually the core of our religions, as you'd think. There is still something that precedes God. Religion came as a response to our notion of God. But God came as our response to the unknown.

This is not to say that God did not already exist independent of our faith, but I'd be willing to bet that what we call God today is much closer to the God we created in response to the unknown than to the real whatever-whoever-God-is.

When it comes to the subject of God or how we came to be, we don't know much more than those people did thousands of years ago. Did this world come to be by a random chain of events or is there a creator? If so, who created the creator? Did the same creator create the sun and all the stars in space? Where does space end? Sometimes we fool ourselves into believing we have the answers to these questions.

"Where does space end?"

"It doesn't. Space is infinite."

"Who created the world?"

"God did."

"Who created God?"

"God is infinite."

Our answers are just more questions in disguise.

In truth, we know very little about ourselves. Within the mystery of how human life came to be, and all the forces governing it, are endless subdivisions of mysteries. How does the heart beat twenty-four hours a day, for a lifetime? What governs the length of a lifetime (why do our cells last just so long)? How can we sleep on our side or upside down and our organs don't smoosh together and stop? How exactly does memory work?

The simple answers are: circulation; human biology; synapses that fire in the mind. But these belie the underlying unknowns.

Does the heart drive circulation or does circulation drive the heart? Its perpetual motion alone is miraculous—unless you want to say it's ordinary. What is going on biologically when you want to recall the name of someone you met once ten years ago? You can't remember at first, but as you think, it's as if you are going through files in your mind, remembering back to where you were, what the circumstances were, digging deeper into details until after a long twenty seconds, the name pops into your mind (or maybe you come so close but then it slips away). These are, of course, subjects it could take a whole book to address. I am a layman asking existential lay questions.

How do our minds not melt trying to understand the concept of a God?

Sanity itself seems like a gift we can easily take for granted. Sanity allows us to live our lives rationally even though we can't comprehend how or why we exist. It allows us to accept God as an answer to the unknown. But sometimes sanity also allows us to take God and the perpetual miracle of our own lives for granted.

The breakneck pace of our modern world seems to leave little time to consider whether what we've been taught about God is true. It is more efficient to pay our dues by spending a short time in a church, temple, or mosque once a week or on holidays, than it is to take the long inward journey required to examine our own belief system.

Living in the present we are naturally aware of our advancement. We get in our car to drive somewhere at night and gaze at the array of lighted instruments and gauges on our dashboard that would have looked like the interior of a spaceship to someone living in the fifties. We can use an earpiece to speak on the telephone—no cords, no hands. We can even issue a voice command to "call Henry," and the phone obeys. We can ask our phone just about any factual question and it will answer. We have global positioning systems that allow us to navigate to an unknown destination. And all these technological wonders will be upgraded to stunning new heights every few years (in the years it took me to write this book I had to alter this paragraph multiple times to keep up with the changes).

Yet, when it comes to our religious beliefs, progress is deemed unnecessary, because we accept without question that our religion is correct in every detail and that we should and must believe it. Religion is the only area of our lives where we cling to what people were thinking and believing two-or-more thousand years ago. Is that because we truly believe that every detail of our beliefs is right, or because we are terrified of risking our souls by being wrong?

Ideally, religion is meant to help us find and develop a

relationship with God. To "find God" sounds oversimplified, or at least so vague that it loses practical value. Nevertheless, to find God has real meaning, even if we can't comprehend God. Shouldn't religion be helping us on our path to learn about God and providing us with spiritual understanding, so that we grow to understand ourselves and the world better with each passing day?

Too often, however, just the opposite happens. Since the ancient beginnings of my religion, we have been fixated on stories of the past. We worship the Bible as a holy book handed down right from the time of Jesus, whose absolute truth we must accept without question, rather than viewing it as a text in service to our spiritual development. In other words, we tend to bow to the book in reverence, rather than believe it is here to serve us, and as a result many people are okay with not knowing more than a few sentences from it.

Many of us believe its stories are factual. Many of us believe all of its words, despite their numerous authors, to have been dictated from God. Yet the stories and the words can be so difficult to understand, even contradictory at times, that what we really end up with as the "divine word" is what our religions have interpreted the Bible to mean.

My Judeo-Christian lineage began when the ancient Jews decided that God created the world and us. Then we began to decide what God wanted of us and how God wanted us to live. We decided what God's words were or were not. Eventually we made what we called God's laws. We claimed that we didn't create those laws or our beliefs about God— God told us what to believe and obey.

The first line of the Old Testament reads: "In the beginning God created the heavens and the earth."[1] This God spoke to a chosen few human beings on earth. He talked to Adam, Abraham, Moses, and a few others. There is no question of there being two distinct parties—God and whomever God spoke to. Moses found God high atop a mountain, where God spoke to him and gave him the Ten Commandments.

This God is separate from us.

We are separate from this God.

Throughout the Old Testament we are told this God must be feared. As mere human beings we must humbly worship God and live by his commandments. It is not our place or within our capability to know the mind of God—much less to question God. If we were to break God's laws, the punishment, we are told, would most often be death.

In the New Testament, we read about Jesus for the first time. Jesus is Jewish, but he preaches from a perspective that differed somewhat from his own religion. For instance, rather than stern commandments in the forefront, he professes the value of love and how each and every individual could enter the kingdom of God. It's not as though the Judaism Jesus grew up in did not speak of love and did not guide the individual to seek God, but there is a shift in focus and emphasis on these matters in the words of Jesus.

Nowhere is this better exemplified than in a passage from the Gospel of Mark. A scribe asks Jesus, "Which command-

1 Genesis 1:1.

ment is the first of all?" Instead of quoting the old scripture exactly ("I am the Lord your God...you shall have no other gods before me."[2]), Jesus gives a more elaborate reply, quoting another part of scripture, "The first is, 'Hear, O Israel: the Lord our God, the Lord is one; you shall love the Lord your God with all your heart, and with all your soul, and with all your mind, and with all your strength.'"[3]

Put more simply, the first commandment according to Jesus is to *love God*. In essence, his answer is no different than that of the Old Testament—to keep God first and foremost in your mind is to love him. But the choice of putting this answer in more tangibly loving terms is no accident—there is an evolution in how we relate to God, but not a replacement, just as an old tree bears new fruit. Isn't Jesus' approach a softening in that understanding of our relationship with God, and doesn't it seem natural? Could it be that we are overdue for a softening in our current religious understandings?

Even more striking support for the shift in emphasis Jesus makes is the second part of his answer to the scribe's question of which is the most important commandment. Jesus goes on to say, "The second [commandment] is this, 'You shall love your neighbor as yourself.' There is no other commandment greater than these."[4]

Love your neighbor is among the most famous messages attributed to Jesus. While the statement could be called one of the pillars of his ministry, these words also come from

---

2 Exodus 20:2.

3 Mark 12:29, which is based on Deuteronomy 6:4–5.

4 Mark 12:31, which quotes Leviticus 19:18. These two commandments from Jesus are also similarly said in Matthew 22:37–40 and Luke 10:27–28.

the Old Testament, although not from the original Ten Commandments. This is remarkably significant because it not only shows him maintaining the old scripture while shifting to a loving emphasis overall, but also because he actually *changed* the original second commandment ("You shall not make or worship any idol"[1]) to "love your neighbor."

It is an important point in our spiritual evolution that Jesus touched the lives of so many through love. People were able to feel the love of Spirit through Jesus. By learning about the love Jesus lived by and with which he treated almost everyone, including sinners, prostitutes, tax collectors, the sick, and the dying, people were offered a way to feel the love of God. Jesus led by the example of loving others, and, because of the many people who have followed his example, that love is still realized in the world today.

(However, I would be remiss if I did not acknowledge that for more than fifteen centuries, through the middles ages and right into the twentieth-first century, there have been those who somehow divorced Jesus from his loving words and examples he set and have violently persecuted those who didn't believe as they do.)

Equally as important as his preaching about loving others, Jesus also preached that all people could find God. Much of his ministry, as told in the Gospels, involved Jesus teaching people how to reach the kingdom of God. And yet my religion, almost from its inception, chose to focus only on worshipping the divinity of Jesus Christ rather than on his teachings. We ignored Jesus' humanity and exalted him exclusively as the anointed one—the special one—the Savior. We elevated and

---

1 Exodus 20:4–5, abridged.

pushed him way up high to the heavens—up, up, and away. And with that came the fear of how to return to him someday.

We have so little about his life recorded, and yet we project details about his lifelong character in his life as a man. Most believers do not want to imagine Jesus as having been anything less than perfect; he is the one and only sinless man who ever lived.

If one day we unearthed an irrefutably legitimate, original Gospel, and it said Jesus as a young man had many years of living sinfully before he began his ministry, would it change your opinion of him? If it said that he sometimes liked to get drunk and tell tall tales would it lessen your respect of him and his words? This is not to suggest these things are true, it is to have you consider for a moment what criteria you use in valuating his words. It can be easy to accept his perfection and thereby just assume his words are perfect too, and subsequently bypass your own learning process as a means to appreciate and benefit from his wisdom and guidance.

The Bible has nothing to say about his ages roughly thirteen to thirty. We fill in the blank of this unknown with our own image of who Jesus was and had to be. He did live as a man after all, could not even the Son of God have been a regular guy who made mistakes or liked to goof around at times? Moving on, let's accept that Jesus was indeed perfect and sinless as a man. This is surely how I like to think of him—I don't try to know the unknowable unknown—it's enough that the ideal gives me something to strive for, and I believe his instruction on how we should live and treat others is one of the greatest gifts of the Bible.

Just as the thought of his perfection can cloud our natural

learning process, it seems the miracles of Jesus are often cherished far more than his words. How often are the miracles of Jesus cited as proof of his divinity? Ask yourself sincerely, if there were no miracles—if Jesus had never walked on water or raised Lazarus from the dead—would your faith be the same? Would you still hear what he had to say?

For many of us who believe in these wondrous stories, there is a temptation to then glaze over the rest of his words as being God's words, yet remove them from the practical use Jesus intended when he sought to teach other men and women how to live righteously and grow spiritually.

Jesus showed us the way to go where he went and to know what he knew. But our own image of and ideas about him, based in large part on the miraculous stories of what he did and who he was, left many of us so transfixed in awe that we could not hear his messages. It's like listening to a beautiful naked woman give a talk on symbolism in Byzantine art— what'd you say?

What the people saw in Jesus was a light beaming like the sun. They felt its warmth, its love, and the spiritual truth that emanated from it. The stories and witnessed accounts of the miracles he performed helped to make the light shine so brightly that people dropped to their knees in worship. And they believed that's all we mortals were meant to do.

Although Jesus beseeched everyone to seek the Father directly, that search took will, inner strength, and endurance, and so, many of us avoided walking that path and were only too happy to accept the fact that it was not our place to do so.

Instead, we worshipped the Son. He came; he knew God; he gave us everything we needed to have spiritually. He gave us the gift of never having to do any spiritual work for ourselves. We didn't have to think anymore. All we had to do was believe in Jesus Christ as our Lord in order to be saved.

First, in the Old Testament, we had a God who existed on high—separate from us. Next, in the New Testament, the Lord descended to earth in human form, but in the end, he too was elevated and separated from us. Jesus stood by God's right side in heaven, and if we held the right beliefs and lived the right life, we were told, we would join them after we died.

Separation from God became even more strongly accepted as our spiritual place.

CHAPTER 4

EGO

The Separate Being

Define ego.

Not so easy, is it?

Dictionaries commonly define ego as the self, as distinct from other selves in the world. Sometimes ego is defined as a sense of self-importance. One with a big ego has a strong sense of self. And when one has an overdeveloped sense of self-importance, we call him egotistical, which is considered an insult to most people.

These characteristics do not, however, fully define the meaning of the word.

There is an underlying spiritual definition created by the belief that you are separate from God. Ego is the part of you that feels outside of God.

Take the case of the people we discussed at the end of the last chapter who were so in awe of the light emanating from

Jesus that they fell to their knees in worship and stopped hearing what he had to tell them. The ego is the shadow created by the separation from that light, and that separation is a belief. Whether we say God, Jesus, the Lord, or Allah—these words describe a supreme deity we look up to and worship as existing somewhere else.

You certainly don't need to believe in God to have an ego. If you don't believe in God, you take your being alone inside as a matter of fact—there is nothing more to you; the ego is simply the self. The psychological implications of this belief are no different from believing in a God that is separate from you—in your thoughts or mental state you perceive yourself as alone.

This sense of being separate has nothing to do with whether you're surrounded by others, in love, in a relationship, or if you have family and friends you love and who love you, nor does it have anything to do with being lonely. Even if you have great faith in God, you likely accept that this life is not the time or place for you to be united with him. For now, you are an individual—"on your own"—and most of us identify ourselves this way. Together, we constitute an ego-dominated world.

A sense of one's own self-importance is not something we commonly associate with spirituality; the ego is not commonly defined in relation to God. In an ego-dominated world, instead of saying, "That guy has a big ego," it may sound silly to say, "That guy has a powerfully fortified illusion of being separate." Yet that is the more precise truth.

Birth of the Ego

As we progress from childhood to adulthood, what is said to us can sometimes affect us as much as what happens to us. We might hear the same things as a child that we hear as an adult, but while adults can choose to keep what serves them and reject what does not, for a child each word is like planting a seed in the soil of who we will become.

As a child you begin to ask questions. The first answers you receive typically come from your parents or the adult who raises you. When it comes to questions about who or what is God, your parents would typically pass on the answers they were taught by their religion, which you then internalize as part of who you are.

It is your parents who first teach you there is a God in the heavens, ruling over your life here on earth and if you believe certain things and behave in certain ways, you will get to be with God in heaven when you die.

A child's mind is not developed enough to understand the ramifications of such profound concepts. On a soul level, however, children know a great deal. When you are taught that you are separate from God there is a powerful latent result. An ego is born.

The Bible tells us that Adam and Eve fell from grace, taking the human race down with them for all time. This is a good way to look at ego; from a spiritual perspective, we are born alone in this world. We are separate from the start.

Ego develops from any perceived separation. A child doesn't need to think about God in order to form an ego. At some point when you were very young you became aware of your thoughts and began to think of yourself as being internally alone. Maybe it happened when you were lying in bed at night staring at the ceiling. Perhaps it was on your first day at school—away from your parents and thrust into an environment full of strangers. You began an inner dialogue that continues to this day.

That first awareness of self is like finding yourself alone in a foreign land. You feel vulnerable, which instinctively triggers you to start developing a way of protecting yourself. When you were lying in your bed at night as a child, that first awareness of yourself may have been experienced as your first fear—fear of the dark. *What is that shape across the room? Are there monsters in the closet or under the bed?* Maybe your young ego found a solution in using a nightlight, which banished the darkness and reminded you that you were in your safe warm room with a parent not far away. Perhaps when you went to school for the first time and felt isolated among strangers, you looked at some kids talking in a group and thought, *How do they know each other already? What if nobody likes me?* You soon found that when you made a new friend or two, you began to feel more at ease because you no longer felt isolated.

The core belief that you are separate and alone, generates all kinds of vulnerabilities, which in turn spin more self-protective thoughts. This ultimately develops into a belief system that dominates your inner dialogue and forms its own sense of who you are. That sense of who you are is your ego, and it takes on a life of its own. This is the separate being inside you. As a child you are not going to have the conscious thought, *I am separate*, but this inner belief still manifests in your thoughts, behavior, and what you say.

Since your ego is part of you, it shares your impulse to survive; the ego wants to live. It must guard your vulnerable self in order to guard itself—to give itself essential purpose to you. It must preserve your identity as a separate being. One of the tools your ego uses for this is, paradoxically, fitting in. How you look to others becomes an important issue. If you stand out in some unusual way, rather than remain anonymous, you may be attacked. It might be only a verbal assault, but words can hurt—they can elicit distress and rock the ego's cozy world.

Take for example what happens in an elementary school playground. Even in the society of children, there is a common understanding of what is "cool" and what is not, especially in terms of style. If someone dresses differently from everyone else, he or she may be teased or bullied or even simply ignored.

Those who have the "right" clothes probably feel secure, while the one who is ridiculed is likely to feel awful and alone. Maybe he will cry and some of his pain gets released. Or he might put a brave face on things in order to protect himself and, of course, his ego.

The children who feel superior, on the other hand, also feed their egos, but their sense of superiority is also separation by another name. They separate themselves from the one kid who doesn't conform, and also prove the vulnerability of their separation by depending on allies for support. Their sense of superiority could be lost in a moment if their circumstances were to change. Whatever your circumstances happen to be, your ego's only concern is that you identify yourself as a separate being, which insures its safety.

Adolescence

By the time you reach adolescence, you have accepted that, on the soul level, you are alone. Your thoughts based on this belief have grown powerful. They run wild and make a lot of noise, and you may live many years believing that noise is who you are.

Your ego still strives to survive and continues its mission to protect you both. It does not want you to question yourself. If you feel alone, sad, or unsatisfied, you might start poking around inside your head to find out why. If you become aware of the separate being inside you and how it causes you to think, you might start to address it. You might want to be rid of it. Introspection is, therefore, a threat to ego. And so, it continues its strategy of having you adapt and blend into your environment as it keeps your attention turned outward.

Do you remember your high school days? You were probably even more concerned with fitting in than when you were younger, and better at achieving it. You could pick something you liked to do and derive the dual benefit of also fitting in. If you were a guy, perhaps you played sports. If you were not athletic, perhaps you fit in with others in band or orchestra, or with those who shared a love of comics, movies, or chess. Some teens found their place with a group of kids who smoked, drank, did drugs, or committed petty crimes for kicks. American adolescence is a time of cliques—groups of peers with shared interests.

The exceptional athletes (the school jocks) were probably popular and got the pretty girls. It might seem that these guys were anything but anonymous. However, we are talking about a system of ego. In terms of ego, they were the stars of the already accepted standard of "normal." They not only met the minimum fitting-in requirement of the ego, but by excelling as they did, they solidified their position within the system. In essence, they rode on the shoulders of all the other members of that system—to cheers and admiration. The status they achieved made their egos (their self-identity) that much stronger. They were kings for the day in the ego realm.

If you were a girl, same principle, just female cliques. If you were athletic, you bonded with other athletic girls. If you were quiet, you probably socialized with other quiet girls. You had the same band, orchestra, debate team, or other types of clubs to feel at home in. You had the same girls who smoked behind the school, or drank and partied more.

You had the exceptional girls too, although the criteria might have been different from the boys. In the school ego system, the exceptional girls were usually the prettiest ones or the ones who developed womanly bodies early. Some of them were cheerleaders and stayed connected to their exceptional male counterparts. They were popular and hung out with other popular girls. They not only fit in but had the boys fawning over them to let them know they were special. They too, being stars in the system, had their egos inflated and strengthened. They were queens for the day in the ego realm.[1]

The star athletes and the prettiest girls were envied by

---

1 The observation of girls/looks in an American high school is not a sexist one—it is a realistic one. Sure, a handsome jock might be the king of the prom. However, for the males of our high school tribe, the emphasis on athletic talent trumps looks. For the females, looks trump athletic talent. At least this was true in the high school I went to. Doesn't some of this mentality carry into our adult culture? Our most popular reality TV shows tend to be based on the mundane details of a beautiful woman's life, not a handsome man.

most of the other egos in school and that perpetuated this system of thinking for everybody. All the different ways kids try to fit in are manifestations of their egos seeking security. The reason cliques develop is because there is strength in numbers; the more you are like the others in your group, the less you stand out.

Trappings of the Ego

The years after high school are a period of transition into adulthood. Whether you go to college, enter the armed forces, or join the workforce, by the time you are a young adult, your ego is highly developed. It is running your life: making your decisions, governing how you feel, telling you how to interpret what happens to you, telling you what is valuable, telling you what success is. Over the years it has become more adept at protecting itself.

As an ego-dominated being, you don't know any other way than to identify with this independent self of yours. Maintaining your peace of mind can be challenging. It seems you are always a victim of whatever adversity life throws at you, and your mental state and emotions are dependent on your circumstances. You may believe in God, go to church, and pray, but God is still up there somewhere, while you are down here on your own. A few of us are born into money, which can cushion us from some of life's adversity, but if you're like most of us, you need to fend for yourself—psychologically, spiritually, and economically.

You (ego) are standing outside in the cold—alone and shivering. This is not a state you wish to be in; it feels uncomfortable. You need a place to live. You need food, water, clothes, health insurance (in America), a car to drive. Money will buy you these things. All of these are realistic survival tools, but they also serve the ego by keeping you stable— keeping it okay to be living "alone" or separate.

One of the most important choices ego has to make for you is how to earn the money you need. Because we live in an ego-dominated society, your ego probably looks at the end goal (money) and works backwards to determine what to do with your life. Generally, as a young adult you pick something you like, or are good at, that will pay the bills. This not only makes life more enjoyable, but helps you fit into society overall.

Someone who has a big ego may not be content to just pay the bills and will desire riches. This is not an arbitrary desire. The ego seeks invincibility, and while paying the bills may provide your basic needs, it still leaves the ego in a precarious circumstance. What would happen if you lost your job? What would happen if anything went wrong? Where would the ego be then? If some tragedy were to befall you, and you were left with no money, you might be deeply afraid. All discomfort and fear lead you back to poking around inside your head and asking questions. That questioning leaves the ego open to exposure, and so it must prevent this by providing for your comfort. The ego wants ultimate security, which (it thinks) comes with a lot of money.

On another note, having a lot of money (what many call success) is the adult version of high school stardom. While the pursuit of riches might not have been his goal in life, the high school "nerd" who pulls up to his twentieth high-school reunion in a Lamborghini, might be crowned the new king.

The Mature Ego

Your ego wants you to feel good and complete with it at the helm. Its job is done to perfection when you are unaware that it is in control—or that it even exists at all. Ego is most secure when you believe ego is simply you.

A woman stands in front of her mirror and thinks, *Do I look good? Is this dress okay?* If asked why she had these thoughts, she might say something like, "I just happen to care about how I look." However, underlying that reasoning is the ego, which has a different agenda. The ego is thinking, *How will I look to others? Will others think I am good-looking?* It is critical for the ego to be accepted by others in order to fit in. If the woman stands out in a way that draws negative attention, she will be vulnerable. If she sees other women whispering or making fun of her, she may feel terrible and might start looking inward for protection. She might subconsciously begin to detect flaws in the ego-system of thought and search for a deeper or higher meaning in her life, which would put the ego in jeopardy.

If, on the other hand, the woman happens to be particularly good-looking, she will also stand out, but in the best possible way for ego. She will not only meet but exceed the criteria for fitting in. She will be admired by those around her, and her separate being will be strengthened. Even if she receives negative attention from those who are jealous, that too will serve to strengthen her sense of self—because, after all, it is her good looks that caused the jealousy. This is why beautiful women (and handsome men) often have big egos.

Good looks, however, can also backfire. Some might automatically assume that because she's beautiful she can't also be intelligent, or that she must have had an easy life. If these (potentially erroneous but stereotypical) judgments upset her, she might become sad or angry, and once again her ego would have to figure out a way to deal with those feelings. In each one of these scenarios, the ego reacts to how she is viewed by others. Whether that is positive or negative, the ego must keep her psychologically secure.

(Incidentally, at this point I should make clear that I have used these stereotypical scenarios as generalizations we can all recognize, and I am fully aware that not all women are so concerned with their looks any more than all men are driven by money. In fact, some men are extremely vain and some women ruthlessly pursue money.)

Any time our insecurities are brought to the forefront of our consciousness the ego must fight to maintain its security, which depends on our having peace of mind. From the ego's perspective, the only solution is a stronger ego. But at some point these battles become tiresome. Maybe we're tired of caring so much about how we look to others—not just physically but in all aspects of our life—our job, career status, how much money we have, our relationships. Maybe we're just exhausted of having to think so much at all.

Perhaps we begin to pray, meditate, or read books, because we've heard there might be a better way (we know inherently there is a better way). We start to pay more attention to our thoughts, to how we're reacting to situations—we start examining ourselves with less ego involvement.

It is difficult to view yourself objectively. Your own thoughts are so familiar to you that you don't commonly observe them. You don't think to think of your thoughts as thoughts. For example, someone rubs you the wrong way and you immediately think, *I can't stand that person*, but maybe you don't delve deeper to discover the source of your animosity. Your ego is quick to react. But every once in a while, you have a moment of clarity—you realize you are the thinker of your thoughts. You can then choose what you think. Can you recall a time when you thought something negative or judgmental about someone for no apparent reason and then stopped yourself in amazement? *Why did I just think that?*

The following example may not apply to you, but for the moment pretend it does. Imagine you're at some social function and someone you barely know comments, "If you have faith in God anything is possible—he can make you overflow with abundance or heal any illness." This really grates on your nerves. You believe in God, and Jesus, but this is just the kind of flippant, spiritual babble that sounds good but has no basis in reality. Besides, it sounds like using God for selfish purposes. You immediately begin to make further assumptions about this person. You find yourself getting angry. Then you realize how ridiculous you're being, getting so wound up over nothing. You look back at this same person (who is still talking) and think, *This guy isn't so bad. What's the matter with me?*

Times like this, when you can interrupt your automatic patterns and look at yourself objectively, are a blessing.

What happened in the case above had nothing to do with the speaker of the words; it had to do with the words and what they meant to you, the person hearing them. The words indicated that you didn't understand something. Since you didn't know if it was true that with faith in God anything is possible, you took the words to mean "You don't really know God," or "You have some lack of knowledge," and that brought up a wave of insecurity.

Your separate being is strong; your ego is powerful. Implying you don't know God might lead to thoughts that cause you to seek further spiritual counsel. This might then lead you to question who you are. It might cause you to ask one of the most threatening questions to the ego: *Do I know God?* This question in turn could lead to a loosening of the ego's powerful hold on you. It could lead you to start praying more earnestly to God for better answers, which in itself diminishes the power of the ego, in order to provide for the possibility of learning something new. You might start seeking out literature in new spiritual areas. You might start to suspect that you need not be separate and alone. You might even start having faith that greater things *are* possible with God.

True or not, in seeking to understand yourself and God better, you threaten your identification as a separate being. Your ego, therefore, summons up opposition to defend itself by blocking out the intruding thought. You remember that Jesus is the Lord and you humbly remember your place. You remember all the words spoken by preachers, family, friends—anyone—that have led you to believe that the person with whom you are now speaking is wrong.

If you should happen to remember later that it says in the

Gospels, "for God all things are possible,"[1] no problem; the ego will remind you that those words applied only to Jesus—only he was truly one with God. There is no foe more wily than a threatened ego.

Often, when you are thinking non-loving thoughts (such as about that stranger speaking about God), the reason for those thoughts lies in the distant past. Let's say, for example, that a little boy got stuck high up in a tree for several hours until someone finally rescued him. Now, as an adult, his thought patterns protect him from repeating that traumatic event. If someone asks him to go hiking up a mountain, his immediate response is to think, *I don't enjoy hiking up mountains*, although he may have no conscious recollection of the event underlying that thought. If you too have automatic responses in particular situations, you can look deeper to see where they come from.

Your anger with the person who is talking about faith yielding worldly rewards came from your ego. To the ego, that man speaks heresy because he speaks about knowing God—he speaks a language opposing separation from God—he is the enemy. Fortunately, you have a big heart and can override the ego's insecurity. You may not be able to agree with what this person said, but you can love him anyway (or at least not hate him).

You'd think it would be a wonderful thing to find God and to learn God is with you. If it is true that anything is possible with God, it would seem to be to your greatest benefit to move closer to God every day. So why would you not abandon the ego immediately? Because, even though it might be wise for

---

1 Matthew 19:26; Mark 10:27; Luke 18:27.

you to break free of its hold, the ego has been with you your whole life—it wants to live and will do anything in its power to survive. Just as an animal with a wounded paw might become ferocious to protect itself, the ego may rise in defense when challenged. And yet, those challenges can be opportunities for growth and finding better ways of thinking or behaving.

The Wounded Ego

Were you ever in a great mood for no apparent reason? Maybe you were doing the dishes or vacuuming the rug and just felt good. Then someone said something unpleasant to you. Maybe someone told you that it looks as if you've put on a few pounds. Or maybe you forgot to do something and your spouse called you irresponsible. You don't feel good anymore, and, as time goes by, your mind keeps gnawing away at the insult and you keep on feeling worse and worse.

First you feel angry that you've been treated poorly. Next, you begin to wonder if the insult actually had any merit and feel bad about yourself. These are manipulations of the ego. It doesn't want you to figure out there is any difference between your ego and yourself because it threatens its control. It wants you to think you are under attack, rather than make the distinction that your negative feelings come from your attacked ego. Your ego wants someone to blame, be it the other person or yourself for being flawed, in order to distract you from realizing that only you choose how you will interpret events and feel. And so, it makes you feel lousy about the other person or lousy about yourself. Ego does not care whether you suffer—only that it is safe.

However, something that shakes us up also tends to have powerful lessons if we do exactly what the ego does not want: get to the bottom of it. We must figure out why, in such a case, we could go from feeling so good to so bad in an instant. If our mood can be changed that easily, it is not because of what someone said to us but because of the weakness of our own foundation, which crumbles as a result.

Let's say it is some young woman's dream to be an actress. Call her Julie and place her in a New York City suburb. Julie lives with her parents while going to acting school. She acts in a lot of community theater productions while working as a waitress to cover her expenses. One day, she finally lands a small role with a few lines in an off-Broadway show. With tears of excitement to share the news, she calls her friends in such exhilaration they can barely make out what she's saying. She is glowing all the way home on the train. She thinks, *I'm finally making it. My dreams are coming true.*

She runs into the house to tell her mother how well the audition went. But her mother, who has never been happy with her daughter's "unrealistic pursuit" of an acting career, just rolls her eyes and says, "But you're a waitress." Almost instantly, Julie's elation turns to despair. She runs to her room and weeps uncontrollably.

What happened?

Once Julie is safely behind the closed bedroom door, head buried in the safety of her favorite pillow, there are two ways her mind can go.

One way is into defense mode. "Mom is such a bitch.

She's jealous of me fulfilling my dreams because she never fulfilled hers. She doesn't understand me at all. I'm talented. The people at the audition saw that. I'm not going to let her do this to me. I'm better than this. I know better." She dries her tears and finds her strength in who she is—a talented actress who just landed a part. Then she calls her best friend, who can commiserate and give support.

In this scenario, Julie rallied to overcome a particular incident. But is she really any the wiser? She has certainly addressed the symptoms—her anger and emotional distress—and is successful this time, but will she be the next? She's like a person with a cough who swallows cough medicine. The symptom is quelled for the moment, but the disease is not cured. Julie has not yet found the root cause of her distress, so whatever it is still lies dormant and ready to flare up again when the right trigger comes along. Since her coping mechanism worked to overcome her distress, perhaps that will become the way she continues to deal with this problem. If her mother's disapproval continues to trigger her loss of composure and confidence in herself, she has to either find the root cause in order to remedy it or stay away from the trigger. If she fails to fulfill her dream of becoming a successful actress, what started out as resentment of her mother could easily turn to blame. Perhaps, sadly, the two will grow further and further apart.

While Julie suffers, however, someone else is celebrating a victory. Someone else just went, *phew, tragedy averted.* It's her ego. At the moment her mother declared "but you're a waitress," Julie lost faith in her own identity. This was the root cause of her distress. She had identified with, and been bolstered by, her success at the audition. Her ego had freshly defined her as talented, on the right career path, an actress in the eyes of others.

Julie had identified with the person the world told her she was, which can only be based on ephemeral circumstantial evidence. Because of that, when her mother then saw her in a different light, Julie instantly doubted herself. As a separate being, she was exposed and vulnerable—caught between two recent pieces of evidence and not knowing which told the truth of who she was (an actress or a waitress). As she fell into a morass of distress, panic, and tears, her ego fought valiantly in its own defense—it retook the helm.

But what if, instead of going into defense mode, Julie became introspective? What if she asked herself, "How did this just happen? Yes, Mom is Mom, but this is my problem. How can I be so sure of myself and then completely lose it like that in a moment? And why can't I let it go? Am I just a waitress? Who am I?"

Ah. The blessed question of questions. The gateway to truth and self-understanding.

Identity

"Who am I?" With honesty and grit, Julie asks the tough question, "Am I just a waitress? Am I simply a product of my circumstances, raised here in this town, the result of my upbringing—my parents and school—all leading up to my job as a waitress? Am I just Julie? Is there nothing more to me?"

She sits for a moment, curious and reflective but almost resigned in her inability to understand. Then, another voice comes into her head. There is an answer coming. "I know there is more to me than this. All the circumstances of my life are true, and who I have become as a result of them is true. I am, in reality, a waitress, yet there is a part of me that is much more. I feel love and a profound sense of knowledge that seems to transcend my age; I feel my soul. My soul knows more than my chattering mind can ever know. What my soul has learned is for keeps, and it is somehow the real me.

"There have been several moments during acting when I felt myself being taken over by the character I played. I would start out self-conscious, but as I let myself just be, and forgot myself, the character seemed to live through me. I seemed to become a vessel for something higher than myself. What they didn't teach me about acting in school is that the more I am able to let go and stay in moments like these, the better an actress I become.

"When I first started out in acting, those moments would come, and I would think what a great actress I was, at which point the magic would disappear. I would forget a line or become myself again, and everyone would see it happening. Wow. Half of acting is the Zen art of surrendering and letting something higher flow through me. When I am able to do that I am something more—I am a soul, I am spirit. I am not just a product of circumstance.

"So why did I get so thrown when Mom said that? I see now it was because I didn't know who I am. Her saying I was just a waitress triggered a lifetime of self-doubt. I felt sad and distressed because I was terrified she might be right. But I see now that I am much more. I feel such powerful love coming through me right now. *What is this?* Is this God?

"And poor Mom—this has been a tough time for her, too.

She and Dad paid a lot of money for me to go to college, and here I am working as a waitress and living at home. She hasn't had an easy life either. Grandma was ten times harder on her than she's ever been on me. She wasn't even allowed to consider her dreams. It was just marriage, kids, end of story. I love Mom."

Julie then goes down to the kitchen and gives her mother a big hug. Her mother collapses in her arms and says, "I'm sorry, baby. I'm so sorry." In that moment they are closer than they've ever been before.

Spirit channels love. Ego channels fear.

Who are you? Are you a product of circumstance? Does everything from your childhood—how you were raised, how loving your parents were, how much money you had—define who you are? What about things that happened to you—maybe some traumatic experience—do they tell you who you are? How about your current life? What do you do for a living, how successful are you, how much money do you have? Are you married? Do you have children? Where do you live? Do any of these circumstances define who you are?

Asking these kinds of questions is your first step toward awakened spirituality (spirit-u-ality; spiritual-reality). Before you can discover who you are, you may have to learn who you are not. If you are an ego-dominated being, as most of us are, you won't be able to fully learn who else you might be unless and until you first realize that you have an ego and understand what it is. But if you will take the time, you can trace every aspect of yourself back to its roots, and you can learn how you came to be who you are in every way.

Having done that, you will discover you are much more than a product of the circumstances of your life. And once you start to realize who you truly are, the days are numbered for the reign of your ego. Chances are, having been dominated by it for so long, it will be difficult to eliminate your ego altogether. We can't all meditate in the mountains for twenty years, or go out to the desert and fast for forty days. We can, however, admit we are egoholics. We can smile to ourselves and say, "My name is ____, and I have a big ego."

Ready to Move On

Do you think I am somewhere else? Do you think, "God is in heaven, but I am down here on earth?" I would rather you know me than believe in me. What is the truth of your heart—do you feel separate from me?

If all or most of the time you feel separate from God, you are governed by ego. But don't worry. To learn such a truth is a grand blessing. You have taken your place among the rare pioneers of Spirit. You have found the door. You stand at the threshold to the realm of Spirit.

You are a spiritual being. It doesn't matter whether or not you know it or believe it. Whether or not you were introduced to God as a child, your soul longs to know the truth about God. You can hear about God ten thousand times and develop a blind faith as mighty as a mountain. Or you can deny there is a God and develop a blind lack of faith as mighty as a mountain.

Either way, at the core of your being, there is a spiritual question you will continue to ask throughout your life: "Is God real?"

This question is asked in many different ways: "Am I alone?" "Is Spirit real?" "Do I have a soul?" "Does God know who I am?" "Does God know I'm in pain?" "Does God know I have bills to pay?" "Will I go somewhere after I die?"

You enter this life with a seemingly blank slate. You probably don't remember anything about your life before the age of three or four. For many years you have no intimate knowledge of anything beyond yourself (no spiritual knowledge of anything beyond your self). The question of whether or not you are alone persists, and there are only two possible answers: Spirit or ego; love or fear. There is a God with you, or there is not. The fear of being alone on a soul level is universally human. No one wants to be alone, but you don't have to be alone, and another person is not required for this to be true.

If you accept on the level of your soul not only that God is real, but also that you are never spiritually alone (God is truly with you), you will have a great comfort. At this time, however, the world we live in is dominated by ego-minded people. Spiritually speaking, this means that most of us believe we are removed from God. We might have some spiritual experiences, but we haven't learned how to live in consistent spiritual awareness. Both spiritually and in reality, the ego is our life.

If you look into your psyche and find *There is just me here, nothing more; God is real, but I am alone while on the earth*, your identity as a separate being seems natural. This is the delusion, and it is a powerful one. It is omni-seductive. It meshes perfectly with the belief that you can't really know

God personally. The ego will vehemently fight to maintain that delusion.

Does the ego truly care about your well-being?

No; its self-preservation is more important than your happiness.

With these understandings, we are now ready to see how the ego relates to religious beliefs.

The following chapters will address the beliefs of the religion I came to call my own, which were my beliefs for many years. My religion taught me to know my humble place as a separate being here on earth; I could be with God only after death, and only if I believed the right beliefs. It taught me that it was not for me to know God and save myself. Rather, it was my asking God's one and only son, Jesus Christ, to be my Lord and Savior that would decide the salvation of my soul. If your religion is like mine, it taught you these things, too.

PART II

CHAPTER 5

THE DOCTRINE OF FEAR

As you read in the introduction, *New Words* was inspired by an experience I had when a voice spoke to my thoughts and addressed troubling questions I'd had about what my religion had taught me. These next four chapters represent more than a decade of my studying and researching the Bible (in the bulk of my spare time from work), as I sought to either corroborate or refute the messages I received.

I will continue, where it seems called for, to quote the voice as it spoke directly to me, in order that it might speak directly to you. So, for example, when you read the words "your religion," please understand that those words were being directed to me. If they do not speak directly to your own religious experience, or if you are not a Christian or do not believe in God, perhaps the words will, nevertheless, provide you with new ways of looking at your own long-held beliefs.

In the introduction, I said the voice spoke as God, a guide, a friend, or as Spirit itself. For this reason, sometimes the voice spoke in the first person ("I" or "me"), and sometimes in the third person ("God"). While this was not confusing for me at the time, I could see where it might seem confusing if I didn't mention it to you here. It's become more clear to me over time that certain points were better served in the more objective sense of the third person, and I also never wanted to change the original words as they came.

Most people who believe in God believe that God is good—God is Love. You would think that religious systems, which worship God, would also maintain that belief. Unfortunately, because of the influence of man's ego, your religion developed with a dark side. Isn't that natural? Ego is the assertion of self outside of God.

Your religion has two sides that cannot be separated. One side contains all the love and spiritual guidance passed on by the one you call Jesus Christ. The dark flipside is all about fear—that you cannot know or ever be with God if you don't accept Jesus Christ as the Lord and your Savior.

Your life on earth has been deemed a trial of faith with eternal ramifications. What happens after death has always been people's ultimate fear. You were offered a way to alleviate that fear with the promise of eternal salvation (heaven), but were also threatened with a more dreadful fear—eternal damnation (hell).

Spiritual bullies—those who command you to believe as they believe and not to question what you are told—have sought to rule your religion ever since its inception. However, you may not recognize the latest evolution of their form. Though the days of bloody proselytizing are over and people are no longer burned at the stake for denying Jesus, the core spiritual belief is still the same: believe or burn—a doctrine of fear.

The entirety of the Gospels—the entire Good News—has been reduced to: you will go to heaven if you believe in the Lord Jesus Christ, which is especially good news based on the alternative.[1]

Hell

Scripture is often cited to support the existence of hell. Yet, when I took the time to examine the scriptures, I found disparities between what the Bible says about hell and what my religion had to say.

Chief among these discrepancies is the main reason you

---

1 The word "gospel" derives from the Old English "godspell," meaning "good news," which is a translation of the Greek word for "good news," as used in the New Testament.

would end up in hell: for not believing in Jesus Christ as your Lord and Savior. Yet you will not find that statement made or expounded upon by Jesus in any of the Gospels, which are the books devoted to his words. If such had been his intention, perhaps there would have been another set of books called "the bad news."

In the Gospels, Jesus did refer to hell, but it certainly was not the focus of his teachings. Nor is the hell Jesus spoke about what most people think of as hell today. But, most importantly, the reasons for going to the hell Jesus spoke about were not based on any of your beliefs. I will show you this through scripture.

Let's start with a quote from the Gospel of Matthew, which is one of the passages you hear quoted regularly in support of the doctrine of fear:

> You that are accursed, depart from me into the
> eternal fire prepared for the devil and his angels.
> (Matthew 25:41)

This is one of the sources for the imagery of "eternal fire" and "the devil and his angels"[1] that permeate our culture. It is a good example to start with, as it is often quoted to show you there is a hell, but the verse is also often taken out of context. You've accepted this hell because it's in the Bible. If you're like me, you assumed the doctrine, which stated you would spend eternity in hell for not holding the right beliefs,

---

1 Otherwise known as demons.

was also founded on biblical authority. But don't you think it would be prudent to research the matter for yourself? In the verses where Jesus talks about hell, the reasons he gave for you possibly going there were based on the judgment of who you were—what you did—how you treated others.

When determining the meaning of scriptural verses, it is important to always look at the surrounding verses. Jesus is talking about a time when a figure called the Son of Man will come to earth to judge all people.[2] We know in this case the Son of Man is Jesus, and he will be the one returning to judge, because in the next chapter of Matthew, Jesus says, "the Son of Man will be handed over to be crucified."[3]

When the Son comes, as king, he will sit on his throne and gather all the people before him. Then he will separate them as a shepherd would separate his sheep from his goats. He will put the sheep on his right hand and the goats on his left. He will tell those on his right that they are blessed by God and shall inherit the kingdom:[4]

"For I was hungry and you gave me food, I was thirsty and you gave me something to drink, I was a stranger and you welcomed me, I was naked and you gave me clothing, I was in prison and you visited me." Then the righteous will answer him, "Lord, when was it that we gave you food, or something to

2 The Son of Man and the Son of God are both titles used for Jesus in the Gospels.
3 Matthew 26:2.
4 Matthew 25:31–34, verses summarized.

drink, or welcomed you, or gave you clothing, or saw you sick or in prison and visited you?"[1] And the king will answer them, "Truly I tell you, just as you did it to one of the least of these who are members of my family, you did it to me."

Then he will say to those at his left hand, "You that are accursed, depart from me into the eternal fire prepared for the devil and his angels; for I was hungry and you gave me no food, I was thirsty and you gave me nothing to drink, I was a stranger and you did not welcome me, naked and you did not give me clothing, sick and in prison and you did not visit me." Then they will also answer, "Lord, when was it that we saw you hungry or thirsty or a stranger or naked or sick or in prison, and did not take care of you?" Then he will answer them, "Truly I tell you, just as you did not do it to one of the least of these, you did not do it to me." And these will go away into eternal punishment, but the righteous into eternal life. (Matthew 25:35–46)

In these verses, Jesus talks about how well you cared for others as the basis for judgment. The cursed people are those who turned their backs on their fellow human beings who were in need, and in so doing turned their backs on God. The righteous people are those who helped their fellow human beings and in so doing helped God. The judgment Jesus speaks about here has nothing to do with believing in Jesus as your Savior.

---

1 Verse abridged.

If you are beginning to feel uncomfortable, bear in mind that what we are discussing in this chapter has nothing to do with your acceptance of Jesus Christ as your Savior, nor am I attempting to define God's judgment as to how to achieve salvation or get to heaven. What we are addressing here is how specific verses from scripture have been improperly co-opted to threaten your soul with hell.

One of the most frightening (and popular) images of hell comes from the book of Revelation:

> And the devil who had deceived them was thrown
> into the lake of fire and brimstone,[2] where the
> beast and the false prophet were, and they will be
> tormented day and night forever and ever.
> (Revelation 20:10)

There are many such verses in Revelation, which have been the sources of dark imaginings in our psyches for centuries. While technically they are different in the Bible, it's pretty common for us to think of the lake of fire as the same thing as Matthew's eternal fire. Revelation then goes on to tell you what could cause you to go there:

---

2 Most modern Bibles translate this now as "fire and sulfur." "Fire and brimstone" comes from the King James Bible, and I use it because it seems to me still the more familiar term in our culture.

and anyone whose name was not found written in the
book of life was thrown into the lake of fire.
(Revelation 20:15)

The "book of life," a term taken from the Old Testament,
appears many times in the Bible. It is the book in which God
lists the names of the righteous. The basis for his judgment is
clarified in a previous verse from Revelation:

Also another book was opened, the book of life. And
the dead were judged according to their works, as
recorded in the books. (Revelation 20:12, abridged)

According to what it says here in Revelation, you will be
judged according to your actions—what you have done (your
works). Here too, there is no link in these verses between hell
and what you believe concerning Jesus. Let's keep exploring
the actual words of the Bible where hell is specifically mentioned, taking them case by case.

The Twelve Verses of Hell

For many centuries, your religion used
scripture to establish that hell existed
and then leveraged the threat of hell
against you if you didn't accept all of its

interpretations of scripture, which took precedence over the actual words. Somewhere along the way, a quantum leap was made from scripture, and hell became the place you go if you don't accept Jesus Christ as your Savior. Every mention of hell in the Bible was then given this understanding, despite what the verses actually said.

It is all too easy to keep repeating the same few verses about hell and make it seem as if the Bible is filled with such verses. It's not unlike seeing the Hollywood set of an old Western town. Looking at the front of the buildings, there appears to be a large town when in fact there is nothing behind those facades; it is all just an illusion.

Do not be misled. The collection of biblical references to hell is not too large or complicated for you to process. In most modern scholar-scrutinized Bibles, the word "hell" is found just twelve times, in its commonly understood use to denote where you'd be sentenced to go by God, if not heaven. Eleven of those times it is Jesus himself who uses the word.

In most of these references, Jesus speaks of being a sinner as the grounds for the judgment that would land you in hell. He issued these warnings in order to help you live a righteous life, and to save you from this fate.

In the first of the twelve verses (which are listed in no particular order), we see again that you are a sinner if you treat others poorly, and it is this sin that could land you in hell:

1) But I say to you that if you are angry with a brother or sister, you will be liable to judgment; and if you insult a brother or sister, you will be liable to the council; and if you say, "You fool," you will be liable to the hell of fire. (Matthew 5:22)

In the second verse, Jesus also warns of the peril of sin. This verse contains a widely quoted biblical description of hell as "unquenchable fire":

2) If your hand causes you to stumble,[1] cut it off; it is better for you to enter life[2] lame than to have two hands and to go to hell, to the unquenchable fire. (Mark 9:43)

One of the most important questions we need to ask is, "What did Jesus mean when he used the word hell?" In the twelve examples that will be listed here, the word for hell comes from the word *Gehenna*, which derives from the Greek version of the Hebrew name of a valley outside ancient Jerusalem where children were supposedly sacrificed by fire.

In the Old Testament, God curses the place, and the people are vehemently warned (upon penalty of death) against worshipping other gods and killing innocent children.[3] Many

---

1 Term for sin.
2 Referring to eternal life.
3 Leviticus 20:2.

centuries later, in Jesus' time, the valley had become a desolate, cursed place in which all the worst refuse of the city of Jerusalem was burned—everything from garbage to dead bodies. The fire was kept going day and night to handle the volume and was, therefore, referred to as never-ending—unquenchable (a smoldering hell on earth).

Did Jesus use *Gehenna* as a metaphor to refer to suffering you would incur if you lived a life of sin, or did he use it as a literal reference for a place of everlasting fire that you could be sent to upon judgment from God? You were likely taught the latter. Over time, the term hell transitioned from any figurative use to being the name of an actual place of eternal torment, existing in another dimension, which you could go to after you die. As the doctrine of fear states: believe or burn.

In the previous example, Mark 9:43, the important message Jesus relays is that you must do anything you can rather than live in sin (even it means cutting your hand off), because dying in sin will mean that you'll go to hell. He is not talking about going to hell for not believing in him. Mark's definition of sin here is likely any action that would keep you from being righteous (in this particular case he was talking about sin as any harm done to "these little ones who believe in me"[4]).

Matthew and Mark use hyperbole several times (cut off your hand, foot, or tear out your eye, depending on which is the cause of your sin), including five more mentions of hell, and of sin being the reason you would end up there. You can scan through these next examples if you like—they all say the same thing. They are listed here so you can see the twelve verses where hell is specifically mentioned, all in one place.

---

4 Mark 9:42.

3) If your right eye causes you to sin, gouge it out and throw it away. It is better for you to lose one part of your body than for your whole body to be thrown into hell. (Matthew 5:29)

4) And if your right hand causes you to sin, cut if off and throw it away. It is better for you to lose one part of your body than for your whole body to go into hell. (Matthew 5:30)

5) And if your foot causes you to stumble, cut it off. It is better for you to enter life lame than to have two feet and to be thrown into hell. (Mark 9:45)

6) And if your eye causes you to stumble, tear it out; it is better for you to enter the kingdom of God with one eye than to have two eyes and to be thrown into hell. (Mark 9:47)

7) And if your eye causes you to stumble, tear it out and throw it away; it is better for you to enter life with one eye than to have two eyes and to be thrown into the hell of fire. (Matthew 18:9)

As you can see, more than half the verses in which the word hell is used have nothing to do with your belief in Jesus. This should be *very* important, shouldn't it? Jesus himself tells you in these verses that sin is what can cause you to land in hell.

In the two verses below, the word hell is used simply in

passing to indicate where the Pharisees and scribes—with whom Jesus is angry—deserve to go due to their hypocrisy. For example, they don't do themselves what they preach for others to do, or they claim to be pious but are only driven by their desire to be recognized as religious authorities.

8) Woe to you, scribes and Pharisees, hypocrites! For you cross sea and land to make a single convert, and you make the new convert twice as much a child of hell as yourselves. (Matthew 23:15)

9) You snakes, you brood of vipers! How can you escape being sentenced to hell? (Matthew 23:33)

Jesus certainly gets into heated exchanges with the scribes and Pharisees, but these verses, too, are not stating that you will go to hell for what you believe or do not believe about Jesus.

The next two examples are parallel verses[1] from Matthew and Luke, in which Jesus is prepping his disciples to go out and spread his messages. He strengthens and encourages them not to be afraid if they are not accepted by people or towns, or if they are persecuted by religious authorities, because God is with them. He tells them, in essence, not to fear those who

---

1 A parallel verse is one that is repeated and virtually the same in more than one Gospel. There may be slight variations from one to another. Parallel verses strongly indicate they both come from the same source.

can hurt them but only to fear God, who has the power to send people to hell.

10) Do not fear those who kill the body but cannot kill the soul; rather fear him who can destroy both soul and body in hell. (Matthew 10:28)

11) I tell you my friends, do not fear those who kill the body and after that can do nothing more. But I will warn you whom to fear: fear him who, after he has killed, has authority to cast into hell. Yes, I tell you, fear him! (Luke 12:4–5)

The last of the twelve examples is the only time in which the word hell is used in the New Testament and is not attributed to Jesus. It appears in the epistle of James (one of the books in the latter part of New Testament). As in the previous two examples, this verse mentions hell, but its main subject is how the tongue leads us to sin.

12) The tongue is also a fire, a world of evil among the parts of the body. It corrupts the whole person, sets the whole course of one's life on fire, and is itself set on fire by hell. (James 3:6)

As you can see, none of the twelve verses containing the

word hell use it is as a direct threat or a consequence of not believing in Jesus as the Lord. The doctrine of fear has been ever based on an unwritten assumption of what the Bible says, which many of us were taught growing up, and throughout our lives.

The Furnace of Fire

Aside from the twelve verses in which the word hell is used specifically, there are others in which Jesus refers to it indirectly or metaphorically (as you've already seen in this chapter). For example, he mentions where "the fire is never quenched." Or, in the verse below, "eternal fire" is used instead of "hell."

> If your hand or foot causes you to stumble, cut it off and throw it away; it is better for you to enter life maimed or lame than to have two hands or two feet and to be thrown into the eternal fire. (Matthew 18:8)

So far we've mostly addressed the believe part of the believe-or-burn doctrine; now for the burn part. If you accept that Jesus referred literally to a real hell, a crucial and hugely underrated question must be asked: When would this hellfire that you've been threatened with occur? Perhaps the answer seems obvious: after you die. But if you read what Jesus had to say about it in the Gospels, you will find that this hell you could go to after you die did not come from Jesus or the Bible. It is nowhere to be found.

Earlier in this chapter, you read a passage from the book of Matthew that spoke about a time when the Son of Man comes from the heavens to judge people and separates them like sheep and goats. The time Jesus was referring to in that passage, however, has nothing to do with a hell you could go to after your particular life naturally ends. Rather, it refers to the occasion of God's final judgment of humanity, which will end the world as we know it—aka, judgment day.

"When the Son of Man comes in his glory, and all the angels with him, then he will sit on the throne of his glory."[1] He ushers in a new age, sometimes called the kingdom of heaven. It is at this time that the sheep will be blessed by God and inherit the kingdom, whereas the cursed goats will go to their eternal punishment.

The entire book of Revelation also refers to this prophesied time and has nothing to do with your individual afterlife.[2]

If you sat in the church I went to on Sunday, you got verses of the Bible thrown at you as you quickly flipped through the pages to keep up with the preacher (if you were so inclined). In a series of quick glances, you saw menacing eternal fires, people being thrown into burning furnaces, and wailing and gnashing of teeth. All that, plus the preacher's message about how to avoid it, no doubt got into your head. The sermon ended, you closed the book, and went home. But

---

1 Matthew 25:31.

2 There is much debate as to what the book of Revelation actually refers to (prophecy, metaphor, or to an ancient time), but you'll be hard-pressed to find any preachers or scholars claiming it refers to an afterlife.

all the while those images played upon your subconscious mind as you went about your daily life.

As for what it says in the Gospels, almost all of these indirect references to the day of judgment, along with their terrifying graphic imagery, appear in Matthew. In Matthew, chapter 3, John the Baptist is blasting the Pharisees with his warning of the "wrath to come;"[3] "every tree therefore that does not bear good fruit is cut down and thrown into the fire."[4] There is no question about what he means. The "wrath to come" is a common biblical reference to the final judgment (along with "day of wrath" and "God's wrath"). And with the wrath comes the fire.

Two verses later, John the Baptist says this message another way as he refers to the proverbial separation of the wheat from the chaff: "He [Jesus] will gather his wheat into the granary; but the chaff he will burn with unquenchable fire."[5]

Then, in a later chapter of Matthew, Jesus states definitively:

at harvest time I will tell the reapers, "Collect the weeds first and bind them in bundles to be burned, but gather the wheat into my barn." (Matthew 13:30)

We don't have to speculate about what Jesus means here. A few verses later, he explains the parable to his disciples, who did not understand:

---

3 Matthew 3:7.

4 Matthew 3:10; this verse is repeated in Matthew 7:19 and Luke 3:9.

5 Matthew 3:12; Luke 3:17.

The one who sows the good seed [that produces
the wheat] is the Son of Man; the field is the world,
and the good seed are the children of the kingdom;
the weeds are the children of the evil one, and the
enemy who sowed them is the devil; the harvest is
the end of the age, and the reapers are angels. Just as
the weeds are collected and burned up with fire, so
will it be at the end of the age. (Matthew 13:37–40)

The wheat and the weeds (or the chaff) are the people
who do God's will and the people who do the evil one's will,
respectively, and they will be separated accordingly at the
time of the final judgment—same meaning as the sheep and
the goats, just a different metaphor.

The same message is repeated twice more and even more
explicitly in Matthew chapter 13:

The Son of Man will send his angels, and they
will collect out of his kingdom all causes of sin
and all evildoers, and they will throw them into
the furnace of fire, where there will be weeping
and gnashing of the teeth. (Matthew 13:41–42)

So it will be at the end of the age. The angels will
come out and separate the evil from the righteous
and throw them into the furnace of fire, where
there will be weeping and gnashing of the teeth.
(Matthew 13:49–50)

And finally, the Gospel of Luke also speaks explicitly
of the time when the Son of Man comes to render God's
final judgment:

> but on the day that Lot left Sodom, it rained fire
> and sulfur from heaven and destroyed all of them—
> it will be like that on the day that the Son of Man
> is revealed. (Luke 17:29–30).

Note that in none of these examples is there anything in-
dicating an afterlife hell you could go to—not the slightest
crumb to nourish that idea. There are, however, specific, in-
controvertible references to the end of this world as we know
it (this age), when the Son of Man comes, and at that time it is
the righteous and evildoers who are separated, not the believers
and nonbelievers. This is the Bible's only timing for judgment
that goes with the understanding of hell as a real place.

So what about all the other references Jesus made to hell
and the fires of hell? There aren't any. Just like that, we've
covered them all. This threat of hell has been grossly over-
stated and misrepresented. The examples in this chapter are
the recycled fuel that has kept the fire raging for all these
ages, and you can still feel the heat on your face today. If
you have any doubts about this timing of hell, you can check
your Bible and see for yourself. If you look objectively at
the scripture, these truths will be self-evident, and you will
be surprised that you never noticed before exactly what the
verses were saying. It will be as if you had walked down a

street a hundred times and never noticed a giant tree that had always been there.

How many of us have been taught the simple proposition, which was said to have come from God, that we either believe in Jesus and go to heaven, or we don't believe and burn in hell? It's not that I'm saying either your religion or mine intended any harm by this. It's simply that these teachings have been passed down for so many centuries, we have all just accepted what we were told. It was even taught that to question the teachings would be damning ourselves to hell.

According to this doctrine of fear, a) the Bible tells us there is a hell; b) the Bible tells us Jesus is the Son of God;[1] therefore, c) if you don't believe in Jesus, you will go to hell when you die. This last teaching is not what the scripture actually says.

There are no verses stating there is a hell you could go to after you die. Nor are there any verses that directly say you will go to hell for not believing in Jesus.[2]

Your faith in Jesus Christ does not demand that you accept all you've been told about hell. You might believe in the hell of scripture, but when you are threatened with warnings about how you could end up there, just make sure you see for yourself what the scripture actually says, and if there is support for that threat.

---

1 Or Son of Man.

2 There are verses stating there will be *consequences* for not believing. We'll get to those in the next chapters.

There is a major distinction between what is written in the Bible and the beliefs formed from interpretation of what is written. If you can find the time, read the New Testament through to the end of Revelation. Separate what is written from what you've been told is meant. Search for your own answers. The matter of your salvation is worth that.

CHAPTER 6

THE SERMON

Like iron dust to a magnet, I always felt drawn to spiritual words. I enjoyed going to church each week. Yet every time I went, some of the things I heard would rub me the wrong way. The sermons usually started out with good words of truth, love, and spiritual wisdom. Inevitably, however, our preacher would circle back to a weekly core message: the reaffirmation of the divinity of Jesus Christ and the ramifications of whether or not we accepted him as our Savior.

We had one main preacher at the church I attended, and a couple of others on staff rotated in on the Sunday service, but the sermons never changed much. Aside from the basic heaven or hell framework, we were reminded that we were sinners— lower, common, flawed beings who, for this reason also, would go to hell when we die. But the good news always followed fast that we could be raised up and saved from this fate through the grace of Jesus Christ—the higher being, the Son of God.

We were told that our spiritual potential to know God was extremely limited relative to that of Jesus, who shared his Father's omniscience and omnipotence. From what I read in the Bible, however, this did not seem congruous with what Jesus taught.

My religion valued a dogmatic adherence to its biblical interpretations—it told us what Jesus' words meant and we needed to believe what we were told. Jesus, by contrast, personified an active spirituality, which he preached for us to have as well—he wanted us to seek understanding for ourselves. His ministry didn't seem to me to be about recognizing our limitations and worshipping him; it seemed to be about recognizing our own potential to build a relationship with God. This led to my eventually learning that religion and spirituality are not the same.

A few years ago, I went back to my church to see if I would have the same experience as I used to. It had been a few years since I heard my preacher preach. Nothing had changed. I heard him say some wonderful things, but I also heard the same teachings that had always struck me as incorrect and even harmful. I recorded that Sunday sermon and have transcribed two important excerpts from it here. This sermon is a good context within which to dig deeper into the doctrine of fear and examine where the Bible actually does link negative consequences to not believing in Jesus Christ.

Perhaps you've heard sermons like this too:

There is nothing complicated about the way to God. The Gospel of Christ is clear, short, and irresistible.

God loves you and wants to have a personal

relationship with you forever. He wants you to grow close to him and spend eternity with him in heaven after you die.

But one thing separates us from a relationship with God ... sin. Sin is disobeying God. The Bible says in Romans 3:23, "For all have sinned and fall short of the glory of God." Romans goes on to explain that the punishment for sin is death—separation from God in hell forever.[1]

Matthew 25:41 tells us that hell is an everlasting fire, prepared for the devil and his angels. No matter how hard we try, we can't save ourselves. We can't earn our way to heaven by being good or going to church.

But don't worry; God loves us so much that he sent his only son, Jesus, to earth. Jesus lived a perfect, sinless life and then died on the cross to take the punishment for our sins. Three days later, he came back to life and now he lives in heaven.

To reach God and live in heaven after you die, you must accept Jesus as your personal Savior and Lord.

Jesus also tells us in Matthew that, "Everyone who acknowledges me before others, I also will acknowledge before my Father in heaven; but whoever denies me before others, I also will deny

---

1 Although the preacher didn't cite the verse number here, he is referencing Romans 6:23. I didn't want to alter any words he said, even to cite a verse number where he didn't.

before my Father in heaven."[1] Jesus is telling us
that to deny him as the most capital sin of all.

This is testified to again by John 15:6, which
says, "If a man does not abide in me he is thrown
into the fire."

Folks, this fate is easily avoided. To accept
Jesus as your Savior, simply talk to God and admit
that you are a sinner, believe that Jesus died for
your sins and was raised from the dead, and give
him control of your life.

If you accepted Jesus Christ as your Savior,
then you can be sure he heard you. Anyone who
calls on the name of the Lord will be saved.[2] You
have just begun a relationship with God and you
will definitely spend eternity in heaven with him.

As I go forward analyzing this sermon, I want to point out
that it is easy for both me as the writer and you as the reader to
fall into the trap of judging the person giving the sermon and
defining him in overly simplistic terms. The wisdom of not
judging others is in part due to the fact that people are rarely
simple to understand or classify.

---

1 Matthew 10:32–33. When typing this footnote, I realized how
impressed we all were and how powerful it was when my preacher,
on a roll, quoted verses from memory, often citing the chapter and
verse number. This contributed greatly to our trust in him as an
authority of scripture and God's messages.
2 This quotes Romans 10:13.

My preacher was a genuinely good and loving man, who wanted to serve God and his congregation. I used to have wonderful talks with him, sometimes for hours. He was my first real guide into scripture and a spiritual mentor for me. As I talk about him in this chapter, my words are intended only to analyze, as objectively as possible, the words that he spoke. It is, in fact, ironic that what troubled me in his sermons inspired me in my lifelong quest for knowledge.

The preacher starts off by saying that God wants to have a relationship with us. He ends by saying that we have just begun one (by calling on the name of the Lord). It is true that he guides us into a relationship with God. However, he makes it clear that the closest to God it is possible for us to get while we are on earth is to know that God is up there in heaven. The majority of his sermon focuses on what happens after you die—as if the whole point of our lives on earth is to prepare our souls for death.

And, what is more, he says that we can't get to heaven to be with God just by being good here on earth—even though this statement directly contradicts Jesus' having said that through our good works we'll be blessed by God and inherit the kingdom ("just as you did it to one of the least of these who are members of my family, you did it to me."[3]). In order to get to God, he says, we must go through his son, Jesus Christ. The stuff of this contradiction is not to be taken lightly and can be a very touchy subject. I am not declaring here that being a good

---

3 Matthew 25:40.

119

person and doing good deeds are the sole criteria for salvation. I am simply pointing out the contradiction between what my preacher said and what Jesus says in Matthew.

While the sermon does its job by offering the way to redemption, it also epitomizes the doctrine of fear. For all its words it has but one message: you must go through Jesus Christ to be with God in heaven and spared from hell.

Why do preachers do this? Assumedly they have already accepted Jesus Christ as their Savior, and most of the people in the congregation have done the same. The answer, they would say, is they are making an argument for the people sitting on the fence (while bolstering the faithful's faith). With altruistic intention, they are passionately imploring souls to be saved. But where in scripture do we find the basis for all the fear linked to what we believe?

Consequences of Not Believing

In the entirety of the four Gospels, there are only eight verses out of the nearly four thousand in which Jesus specifically refers to there being consequences for not believing in him, which have been interpreted to mean you will go to hell.[1] Relative to the text as a whole, the subject is hardly mentioned at all.

The first example of a verse commonly bent to this purpose (and shown in the sermon) has caused great controversy over the ages and is still wreaking havoc today.

---

1 Three of those are the same verse repeated in three Gospels (parallel verses), so actually there are only six different verses.

> Whoever does not abide in me is thrown away like
> a branch and withers; such branches are gathered,
> thrown into the fire, and burned. (John 15:6)

Having been conditioned to fear, all one has to do is glance at this verse, or hear it quoted, to interpret it to mean: believe in Jesus or else...

To begin with, pay attention to what you think and feel when you read the word "fire." The association of fire with hell is so strong that it's easier for you to accept the fear than to search for the meaning. As with many verses in the Bible, it's possible that this one is not meant to be taken literally. But even if there is only a small chance that the word fire is referring to hell, you might think, *why take the chance?* It's easier to just believe so you'll be okay.

Can fire ever be just fire? Jesus did use metaphors often in order to get his points across. For this reason, the more familiar you are with the Bible and its language the more data you will have upon which to decide context and meaning. Take a look at these beautiful verses from Matthew, which also appear similarly in Luke:

> And why do you worry about clothes? See how
> the lilies of the field grow. They do not labor or
> spin. Yet I tell you that not even Solomon in all
> his splendor was dressed like one of these. If
> that is how God clothes the grass of the field,
> which is here today and tomorrow is thrown

into the fire, will he not much more clothe you,
O you of little faith?"
(Matthew 6:28–30; Luke 12:27–28)

The phrase here, "thrown into the fire," clearly refers to something transitory—here today, gone tomorrow—not the fire of hell. Just because thrown into the fire means hell in one place does not mean it has to have the same meaning in another. These references to the transitory nature of life are common in biblical language.[1] In another well-known verse of Matthew:

You are the salt of the earth; but if salt has lost its taste, how can its saltiness be restored? It is no longer good for anything, but is thrown out and trampled under foot. (Matthew 5:13)

In other words, the salt without its flavor has no value and can be thrown away. If instead of "thrown out," Matthew had said here, "It is no longer good for anything, but is thrown into the fire," the salt's flavor probably would have been equated with belief in Jesus for all the ages.

So, in John 15:6, when Jesus spoke of branches being thrown into the fire, did his metaphor refer to you literally being thrown into the fire of hell? Or did he mean something else? If you look

---

1 "Grass" especially is used as a metaphor for transitory in this regard several times in the Old Testament Psalm 37:2; 90:5–6; 102:11; 103:15–16; 129:6; Isaiah 37:27; 40:6–8; 51:12; Job 8:12; NT: 1 Peter 1:24.

at John 15:6 in the context of the preceding verse, Je

> I am the vine, you are the branches. Those who
> abide in me and I in them bear much fruit, because
> apart from me you can do nothing. Whoever does
> not abide in me is thrown away like a branch and
> withers; such branches are gathered, thrown into
> the fire, and burned. (John 15:5–6)

The fear of hell distracts from two salient points here. First, every other time Jesus speaks of your being thrown into the fire in association with hell, he is referring to judgment day. Second, and more importantly, to focus only on the fearful, literal interpretation is to ignore a rich lesson offered by the verse. If you're terrified of the dirt, you're not going to dig for the gold.

Jesus is speaking about having his spirit and his teachings running through your veins (abiding in God) and what that means for the strength and integrity of your being. Conversely, without God's spirit and teachings, you are a dried-up branch connected to no vine—no source—that, of course, withers, and what do we do with withered up branches and twigs? We gather them and throw them away or burn them in our fireplace.

There are other verses in the Gospels that are similar to those, but because their metaphors do not involve fire, they are not as commonly appropriated to support the doctrine of fear. In parallel verses in Matthew and Luke, Jesus says:

Everyone then who hears these words of mine and acts on them will be like a wise man building a house, who dug deeply and laid the foundation on rock. When a flood arose, the river burst against that house but could not shake it, because it had been well built. And everyone who hears these words of mine and does not act on them is like a foolish man who built his house on sand. When the river burst against it, immediately it fell, and great was the ruin of that house.

(Matthew 7:24–27; Luke 6:47–49) [1]

Jesus relays this message other times using a variety of metaphors. Here he calls his teachings a good foundation on which to build your house. Are those words so different from those describing the branches that are full of spiritual life or dead inside, depending on whether or not they are attached to the main vine (the good Source)? In the Gospel of John, he puts this yet another way, "I have come as a light unto the world, so that everyone who believes in me should not remain in the darkness."[2]

Metaphors can often elucidate spiritual matters better than direct speech—in much the same way that poetry can communicate subtle ideas better than plain prose.

Obviously Jesus was not referring to your building an actual house, or to an actual river that would crash against it, or that without his light you'd remain in darkness in a room

---

1 The two Gospels parallel each other closely, but are different, and my citation here borrows elements from both.

2 John 12:46.

in your house. But just as not everything he says is meant to be taken literally, not everything is meant metaphorically either. You must consider every example individually and decide for yourself. Don't just accept what others tell you the words mean, and don't let everything get homogenized into a common mix that obscures what each verse means on its own.

The Reduction of Scripture

Absolutes are weapons used by the doctrine of fear. The doctrine wants to reduce all verses, whenever possible, to mean that you either believe in Jesus or you don't, and, as a consequence, you are going either to heaven or to hell. But the doctrine on its own has no power. It needs an ally to do its work. It needs your ego. It needs the part of you that doesn't want any ideas to conflict with what you've been told is the truth. Namely, that you are a being who is separate from God and though God is aware of you, you cannot know God—not really—not until you die, so you better believe rightly and be ready if death (or a judgment day) should come.[3] Your ego wants you to be comfortable in your separation; it wants you to feel safe so it can feel safe. It therefore uses your greatest fear—that if you don't believe you will burn—to keep you from searching further for spiritual truth.

Because this fear runs so deep, your ego can lead you to believe that to even question a verse that speaks about Jesus is to somehow to deny Jesus. The implication is that to question anything is to question everything. But believing in what a

---

3 Keep awake therefore, for you do not know on what day your Lord is coming. (Matthew 24:42)

verse means and belief in Jesus Christ are two distinct issues.

Again, the divinity of Jesus Christ is not at issue here; the only issue is how certain verses are stripped of deeper meaning and used as absolute threats. Jesus' words offer us a vast amount of spiritual wealth and well-being, if we can only free ourselves from being trapped by the belief systems and understandings of men from ancient times.

> Your religion is obviously not a malicious body intending you harm. It is simply mired in the ghosts of its predecessors, who understood me only in terms of fear. These eternal threats of damnation can make you afraid to question what you've been taught.
>
> You should question anything you've been taught. Research and seek the answers, in order to know for yourself whether what you've been taught is valid. You have nothing to fear and everything to gain in solidifying your faith through knowledge. Only your ego has everything to fear and everything to lose from your breaking free of its threats and dominion over you.

The second example of a verse commonly interpreted to mean that hell will be the consequence for not believing in Jesus is found in the Gospel of Matthew. This verse of scripture is quoted in the sermon and we heard it regularly at church (the third and fourth examples are parallel verses of this teaching found in Mark 8:38 and Luke 12:8–9):

Everyone therefore who acknowledges me before others, I also will acknowledge before my Father in heaven; but whoever denies me before others, I also will deny before my Father in heaven.
(Matthew 10:32–33)

Traditionally, these verses are taught to mean that if you deny Jesus you won't get into heaven after you die, with the further implication that you will go to hell—although the latter goes *without saying*. Remember how strongly your fear can influence your understanding. As with the previous example, the dogmatic approach is an attempt to make all scripture susceptible to just this one interpretation. Maybe that interpretation is true. The debates can never be settled, but the truth is yours to find. For your consideration: its meaning could be similar to that of the verse about the branches that appears in John. There, by abiding in Jesus your life would bear fruit; here, you benefit by acknowledging him.

If you want to accept the plain meaning that if you deny Jesus you'll be denied entrance to heaven, there is still no avoiding the fact that this verse refers to what will happen on judgment day, not when you die. This is clearly shown in the parallel verse in the Gospel of Mark: "Those who are ashamed of me and my words in this adulterous and sinful generation, of them the Son of Man will also be ashamed when he comes in the glory of his Father with the holy angels."[1] This judgment day, heralded by the Son of Man coming with his angels, has been understood and preached from day one in almost all religions in Christ's name to refer to the end of the world as we know it.

Romans

The book Romans, which follows shortly after the Gospels in the New Testament, is one of the letters written to nascent Christian churches from the apostle Paul, who spread the messages of Jesus in the first century (these are also called the epistles of Paul). These letters addressed various beliefs of the new Christian people, laid a foundation for, and were instrumental in the dissemination of Christianity. Paul's writings are also considered by scholars to be the oldest in the New Testament.

Romans has a deeply invigorating exposition on sin, which instructs you as to what sin is and your personal responsibility to stay aware of it, while also prescribing Christ as the remedy to rise above it. In the sermon, a couple of Roman's more popular verses were reduced and made to serve only the dogmatic, fearful teaching of Godly judgment.

Look at how Romans is quoted in the sermon:

> The Bible says in Romans 3:23, "For all have sinned and fall short of the glory of God." Romans goes on to explain that the punishment for sin is death—separation from God in hell forever.

---

1 Mark 8:38.

The preacher here pulls the first verse out of its context and attaches it to the second verse (from Romans 6:23) in order to support his own declared meaning: You are a sinner who is predestined for hell unless you choose Jesus to save you. As he later says, to deny Jesus is the most capital sin.

A preacher has your trust, and, as a man who serves God and spends his life studying the Bible, it seems fitting to accept what he says. But while my preacher had good intentions, it is a dangerous practice to mix and match verses of scripture. The full statement, of which Romans 3:23 is a part, says:

> since all have sinned and fall short of the glory of God; they are now justified by his grace as a gift, through the redemption that is in Christ Jesus. (Romans 3:23–24)

The verses state what is said many times in the New Testament: Your sins are forgiven through Jesus Christ, which is to say, your belief in him. The verse does not, however, in any way define sin as not believing in him, or link not believing to hell; only the mix-matching of verses out of context alter the meanings in these ways.

As you read in the last chapter, the Gospel of Matthew speaks a lot about sin and how it could land you in hell. But there is a major difference between what Romans has to say about sin and what is written in the Gospel of Matthew. Whereas in Matthew you can choose through your actions whether or not to be a sinner, Romans states that you already are and have always been a sinner.

Romans features a definition of sin and redemption based on past and present, comparing Adam to Jesus. The state of grace (or glory of God) was lost through the sin of Adam and continued evermore through successive generations. There is no getting around this fact, as the preacher reminds us in his sermon. You can be the most righteous person on earth. You can be a truly selfless soul whose only devotion is to helping others, but, as Paul says another way earlier in Romans, "All are under the power of sin, as it is written: 'There is no one who is righteous, not even one.'"[1]

In other words: everyone is a sinner. Sin is your birthwrong.

Romans tells us that Jesus forgives that sin and allows humankind to be restored to God's grace through him. The text does not say: "All sinners without Christ shall go to hell." However, you can see how easily that assumption might be made. This is the same old formulaic assumption we've already discussed, but it's worth repeating because there are few issues so vital to your well-being. You see in one place (for example in Matthew) that there is a hell you could go to for being a sinner.[2] You see in another place (here) that sinners can be redeemed through Jesus Christ. Then the math is done for you and what it adds up to is that if you don't accept Jesus Christ you will go to hell. This is the negative assumption, outside of scripture, which we discussed in the last chapter.

While Romans 3:23–24 says nothing about hell, it does

---

1 Romans 3:9 (abridged); Paul quotes Ecclesiastes 7:20 in the Old Testament.

2 "If your right eye causes you to sin, tear it out and throw it away; it is better for you to lose one of your members than for your whole body to be thrown into hell." (Matthew 5:29)

say you are justified through God's grace and can be re‹
through Jesus Christ. If you shake off the negative assumption, the
verse says something powerfully good. It focuses on the positive
(your redemption); with Christ comes everlasting good. This
seems to be the most important message Paul wants to convey.

In the quoted sermon, as in countless other sermons people
hear, the preacher takes excerpts from various verses to focus
on and prove your lowly nature. Then there are always the
two absolutes to choose from: you can either remain the lowly
sinner you are, or you can be saved.

> Jesus focuses on what you gain through atten-
> tion to your spiritual life—to living a righteous
> life. Your religion focuses heavily on the
> negative—what you lack—and the terrible
> place you might go as a result.

Romans 6:23, cited in the sermon, is another example of a
verse that has been used to induce fear: "The wages of sin is death,"
which the preacher further defines as "separation from God in
hell forever." This, however, is not what the verse actually says:

> For the wages of sin is death, but the free gift
> of God is eternal life in Christ Jesus our Lord.
> (Romans 6:23)

It does a major injustice to the verse to leave off the second half it, and this is again mis-matching verses of scripture; however, there is a much more important issue here: the meaning of "death." How the word death is preached about here is another example of crossing the line between what is written and what is inferred. The verse says the wages of sin is death, not hell.

Death does not mean hell. If you read this whole chapter in Romans for context (or, better yet, read the whole book of Romans), you will see that nowhere is death associated with any of the language referring to hell that is found elsewhere in the Bible, such as eternal fire or lake of fire. Nor will you find the word hell in any of the verses that talk about death.

Death is a word that has two meanings, both of which are discussed in Romans. There is the literal meaning of physical death, but the bulk of Romans discusses a more profound spiritual meaning. Death is the state of separation from God (or separation from the kingdom of God). However, equating that separation with an eternal afterlife in a physical place of torment and suffering is, again, a leap beyond what is written.

Chapter six in Romans speaks about your spiritual life with or without Christ. Verse 6:23 says again what is found in the Gospels: with God, spiritual life is in you; without God, there is no spiritual life (death). It is not talking about an afterlife; it is talking about your current state of being, based on your acceptance of God and his words, which, according to Paul in Romans, means based on your faith in Jesus Christ, his words, and his works.

"Sin" is usually thought of literally, as a wrongful or unrighteous act (defying God), which is harmful to ourselves or others. However, sin is another word that has a spiritual definition underlying its literal meaning. In this sense, it is anything that separates you from God. It is the act that puts you in spiritual death. By choosing sin in any of its many forms, you are denying the grace of God; you choose to be separate from God. This is not a choice whose repercussions come later. It is a choice that affects your life now.

If the ramifications of faith and righteousness, or lack thereof, occurred only after physical death (if, in other words, the spiritual realm were reserved for the afterlife), forgiveness of sin would not exist in the world. It could be waiting for you only after you die—if you had faith. And if you didn't have faith or lived in sin, you would not experience the consequences of that until you died. But the scripture says the spiritual life is flowing through you. The question is, will you accept it or deny it? As soon as you heed the words of God—learn the lessons the Bible has to offer—you tap into the spiritual life flowing through you and throughout the world. Deny the words—ignore the lessons—and you cut yourself off from that source. The price of sin is separation from God.

How cutting yourself off from God might relate to any future judgment is another matter but, in Romans, Paul is quite clear on what will happen on the day of judgment and when it is:

> But by your hard and impenitent heart you are
> storing up wrath for yourself on the day of wrath,[1]

---

1 This biblical term for God's judgment can be found many places; Job 20:28; 21:30; Proverbs 11:4; Zephaniah 1:15; 1:18; Isaiah 13:9; Psalm 110:5; Ezekiel 22:24; Revelation 6:17 ... to name just a few.

when God's righteous judgment will be revealed.
For he will repay according to each one's deeds:
to those who by patiently doing good seek for
glory and honor and immortality, he will give
eternal life; while for those who are self-seeking
and who obey not the truth but wickedness,
there will be wrath and fury. (Romans 2:5–8)

Not only does Paul define God's wrath in similar terms as we see in Matthew's Gospel, he also mirrors here the essential message of God's criteria for judgment that Jesus preached throughout Matthew, Mark, and Luke. Do you not think Paul, perhaps the most influential figure in the founding of Christianity, knew what he was talking about? These verses showcase the pure virtues Jesus spoke of—"pure" describing not any belief you have but rather the measure of who you are, and wickedness defined as sin and caring only about yourself—not a lack of belief in Jesus.

Whether you want to believe judgment comes at the end of your life or at the end of the world, the notion that you have only two options: eternal life in heaven or eternal separation from God in hell, means that the only important teachings in the Bible are those that pertain to this terrifying choice. It evokes the blinding temptation to close your mind and ignore the spiritual value of everything else written in scripture.

Rather than studying the Bible and seeking to grow spiritually, you can become preoccupied with only those few sentences you are told will decide your fate. The Bible does not exist simply to prop up a few key statements from God. You are not meant to read the Bible as something that is beyond your ability to comprehend. Rather you are meant to interact with what it says. One of the reasons the Bible is eternally relevant is that its words are alive and speak to you intimately. You walk and talk with a living God as though you were there. When Jesus talks to his disciples, he talks to you. When Jesus advises someone how to find the kingdom of God, he advises you. His messages are intended to wake you up and make you aware of Spirit, not to put you to sleep and make you ready to be with Spirit when you wake from death in heaven.

No one can determine what is true for us all, but you have the power to seek God's truth for yourself. Jesus calls upon you to follow him and to find the kingdom of God for yourself. His mission was to awaken you to your potential and offer you a path to salvation. His messages were meant to ignite and propel your soul upwards. Having a relationship with God was not/is not for religious authorities alone; it was/is for everyone. Keep searching for the highest good news. It is for you. It is you.

Listen to Jesus

In the Gospel of John, Jesus radiates his purpose: to make you aware of God, to show you that you can know God, and what this means for your life.

Then Jesus cried aloud: "Whoever believes in
me believes not in me but in him who sent me."
(John 12:44)

Believe me that I am in the Father and the Father
is in me; but if you do not, then believe me
because of the works themselves. (John 14:11)

There is a point in the second verse that is easy to over-
look. Jesus is telling you: *Do not trouble yourself if you cannot
see who I am at this time. If nothing else, just look at the things
I've done and decide if you see God in them, and therefore in
me.* If Jesus can suggest (even once) that you are able to find
the truth of who he is through his works rather than by being
threatened with terrible consequences for not believing in him,
how can you allow anyone else to lay such absolute threats
upon you?

And if that were not enough, Jesus gives you more than
you could ever have expected:

Very truly, I tell you, the one who believes in me
will also do the works that I do and, in fact, will
do greater works then these, because I am going
to the Father.[1] (John 14:12)

---

1 Meaning he is going to be dead soon and back with God.

How could you ever do greater works than J

Because, unlike a belief system that wou

down, mired in the negativity of your limits, J

you to see the unlimited possibility in your relat

God and your ability to do great works. Will you deny his words? How loving he is while passing on this most valuable information to you. Do you believe he said these things just to be a nice guy? He is telling you, *I'm leaving this world, now it's your turn, and you know what? You will do things the world has never seen before—beyond what I did— because you are a unique person living in the world, now, who through you own seeking and perseverance will build upon what has come before.* The Lord is humble while focusing on your potential greatness. So how does any religion created in his name come to focus so heavily on your innate deficiency?

Jesus focused on who you are and the works you can do while alive. Your religion focuses on who you are not and what happens after you die.

The doctrine of fear can have you so deeply entrenched in the absolutes of "you either believe or you don't," that you may not realize there is another perspective: a doctrine of love. Leave all the debates about hell behind for a moment. Do you believe in God? Do you believe God loves you? What do you really believe about the nature of this God? Is he a God to fear or a God of love?

If you believe God loves you, and you believe God is

perfect, would he have hidden the risk of your burning in hell for eternity in mixed messages that could be saying one thing or another? All it would have taken is one or two sentences stating something like: "You shall know the everlasting fires of hell as soon as your life on earth ends if you didn't believe the right belief." Or, "Be careful not to live in sin, for if you die a sinner you will immediately go to the place of eternal fire and torment, where the devil and his angels live."

The essential question is, do you really suppose that a God who loves human beings as his children—who loves you—could ever sentence you to burn in an eternal fire? Tabling grievous sin for now, do you suppose God would torture you eternally for any number of sins you might rack up in one lifetime? If you have never committed a sin, if you did nothing but help the poor, sick, and needy, but you didn't believe the right beliefs, would God drown you in a lake of fire forever? And even if God were to dispense such eternal punishment, what would be the point? How would that benefit you or God? Why would he bother?

As you get swept up in the drama of absolutes—accepting as a given that this doctrine of believe-or-else is true—you don't stop to examine what's behind that choice or where it came from in the first place. One thing is certain: the greatest fear people had two thousand years ago—of God's judgment and punishment—is alive and thriving, relatively unchallenged to this day.

Have we not come of age to let go of these beliefs? Are the dark ages not over? Can we be the generation to break free of these ancient fears? Can we cleanse our spirituality—our relationship with God—of all the negativity?

CHAPTER 7

WORDS OF LOVE AND SEEKING

The Gospels are filled with much more than the few verses exploited by the doctrine of fear. It would take too much space here for me to list all the words of love, light, guidance, and wisdom in the Gospels. Instead, I have listed some of the catchphrases from these numerous verses. These are verses you can ponder for a lifetime, glean new meanings as you grow, and grow with the new meanings. You can feel love and learn about love through these words. Even if you are not very familiar with the Bible, you will probably recognize many of these, as they have permeated our culture for centuries. Instead of just scanning the list, actually read each line to yourself.

Love God.[1]
Love your neighbor.[2]

_____

Mt=Matthew; Mk=Mark; Lk=Luke; Jn=John
(1) Mt 22:37; Mk 12:30; Lk 10:27. (2) Mt 22:39; Mk 12:31; Lk 10:27.

139

You are the light of the world.[1]

Let your light shine. [2]

Love your enemies.[3]

Bless them that curse you.[4]

Pray for those who abuse you.[5]

Pray for those who persecute you.[6]

Do good to those that hate you.[7]

If you are angry with a brother or sister, you will be liable to judgment.[8]

Be you perfect [in your love] as your heavenly Father.[9]

Love one another as I have loved you.[10]

If anyone strikes you on the cheek, turn the other also.[11]

Do not judge, so that you may not be judged.[12]

Do not condemn, and you will not be condemned.[13]

Ask and it will be given to you.[14]

Seek and you will find.[15]

Knock and the door will be opened to you.[16]

Do to others as you would have them do to you.[17]

Be merciful, just as your Father is merciful.[18]

Forgive, and you will be forgiven.[19]

The truth will set you free.[20]

Those who humble themselves will be exalted.[21]

If you have faith you can move mountains.[22]

---

(1) Mt 5:14. (2) Mt 5:16. (3) Mt 5:44; Lk 6:27. (4) Lk 6:28. (5) Lk 6:28. (6) Mt 5:44. (7) Lk 6:27. (8) Mt 5:22. (9) Mt 5:48. (10) Jn 15:12; 13:34. (11) Mt 5:39; Lk 6:29. (12) Mt 7:1; Lk 6:37. (13) Lk 6:37. (14) Mt 7:7; Lk 11:9. (15) Mt 7:7; Lk 11:9. (16) Mt 7:7; Lk 11:9. (17) Mt 7:12; Lk 6:31. (18) Lk 6:36. (19) Mk 11:25; Lk 6:37. (20) Jn 8:32. (21) Mt 23:12; Lk 14:11.(22) Mt 17:20; 21:21; Mk 11:23; Lk 17:6 (though Luke uses "Mulberry tree" instead of mountain).

Don't be afraid, just believe.[23]

For God all things are possible.[24]

Whoever does not receive the kingdom of God as a little child will never enter it.[25]

Whatever you ask for in prayer with faith, you will receive.[26]

Give, and it will be given to you.[27]

So do not worry about tomorrow, for tomorrow will bring worries of its own.[28]

Most of these kinds of phrases, which are intended for your personal spiritual instruction, come from the first three Gospels (Matthew, Mark, and Luke). As you read these Gospels, you find that they have common themes, similar stories, and many of the same sayings. For this reason, the first three Gospels are often referred to as the Synoptic Gospels.[29] In the Synoptic Gospels, Jesus hardly mentions what you ought to believe about him. Rather, he talks a great deal about the value of your faith in God, the importance of loving others,[30] and offers numerous ways to help you learn about the kingdom of God. In these Gospels you read about what being a good person means to Jesus and how to apply his spiritual lessons to

---

(23) Mk 5:36. (24) Mt 19:26; Mk 10:27; Lk 1:37. (25) Mk 10:15; Mt 18:3; Lk 18:17. (26) Mt 21:22. (27) Lk 6:38. (28) Mt 6:34. (29) The term comes from the Greek word *synopsis,* meaning "to be seen together." Due to their similar stories, content, and layout, you can easily compare them to see how alike they are (and also where they are different). (30) Most of the messages about loving others are found in Matthew and Luke.

eryday life. The Gospel of John, however, is fundamentally different from the Synoptics in that it does tell you what you need to believe. It focuses on the divine identity of Jesus Christ and the salvation you'll gain from believing in him.

In the previous two chapters we discussed the few messages—some of them beyond the scope of scripture—that religions like mine have focused on to instill the doctrine of fear. In this chapter, I summarize the themes of love and seeking that are found in so many of Jesus' messages. All the words of Jesus discussed in this chapter will be from the Synoptic Gospels. The Gospel of John will be the subject of the next chapter.

There are many themes in the Gospels and many complicated issues surrounding what Jesus said and did and the interpretations of his words. This chapter is not meant to be blindly idealistic or to make the argument that these themes of love and seeking are the only kinds of words to which we should pay attention. Rather, my purpose is to provide you with evidence of how often these positive themes occur throughout the Gospels, in order to make you see how much more weight they deserve in our understanding of what the ministry of Jesus was about—to show that love was the heart of him and all he said and did.

Love

When you read through the list of phrases earlier in this chapter, did you understand what each one meant? For fun, try to answer this question out loud: what does it mean that you are the light of the world? Or, why will the humble be exalted? These are spiritual sayings, as are the others on the list.

Perhaps you agree they are the words of God. Spiritual sayings are understood intuitively. For example, you understand intuitively that, in the first saying, "light" refers to your soul, your goodness. To let your light shine in the world is to bring joy to the world with your love, your smile, your good will to others. Over time, your own life experiences can contribute to the depth of meaning the words have for you personally.

As for the humble being exalted, you probably know that being humble is a virtue. This saying is a loving instruction, because being humble will help you to learn, to grow, and to know God. Humble people are on their knees, so to speak, and don't think they know everything. They are open and ready to learn. Humble people are open to receiving spiritual information. Those who think they know everything have no room to be taught any new information. Because they believe they already have all the answers, they miss what information God might have for them. This can lead to all kinds of pain and failure, which being receptive to God's ever-new lessons (even based on his old words) might have averted. And so the verse begins: "All who exalt themselves will be humbled, and all who humble themselves will be exalted."[1]

Your understanding of spiritual words is enhanced by the knowledge you gain through your personal experience with Spirit (or personal relationship with God). Let's say that one day you saw an old man struggling to carry his groceries to his car. Without thinking about it, you immediately went to help him. After, as you watched him drive away, a deep pleasure swept through you. You learned that helping someone in need feels good—your satisfaction came from his benefit. Henceforth,

1 Matthew 23:12; Luke 14:11.

you have the spiritual knowledge that there is reward in caring for others. Perhaps you will also realize that this is the kind of world you want to live in. You understand better why Jesus preached for you to love your neighbors.

Jesus knew that we are beings of love and when we treat other people with care, we are living in harmony with our true nature. We can debate biblical interpretation, religion, philosophy, or even what "good" is, but no matter whether it came from God or is something we learn for ourselves, love suits us. It feels good to hold open a door for someone else. It feels good to help someone in need. It feels good to love others. It feels good to be loved. "Be good to one another" is a teaching we can all feel in our hearts to be righteous—whether we are religious or not, and whether or not we believe in God. All of this is only true, of course, for each of us who endeavors to be what we generally think of as a good person.

Jesus teaches you how to spread love in the world. He tells you how to practice loving your neighbor as yourself (i.e., how to live in harmony with who you are), and how to do what you are told is God's will in the world: forgive others; be merciful as God is; don't be angry with others; don't judge or condemn people; treat others as you would have them treat you.[1]

You are told to be as perfect in your love as God is in his. Normally, you love your family and others who love you. But to be perfect in your love, as Jesus says, you must also love your enemies or those who harm you. If someone strikes you on the cheek, turn and offer him the other cheek. There is a model for ethical, moral, and righteous behavior laid down in these Gospels, and that model is founded on love.

---

1 These ideals are based on the list at the beginning of the chapter.

Take a look at some of what Jesus says in his famous Sermon on the Mount, in the Gospel of Matthew.

How blessed are:
the poor in spirit, for theirs is the kingdom of heaven;
those who mourn, for they will be comforted;
the meek, for they will inherit the earth;
those who hunger and thirst for righteousness,
    for they will be filled;
the merciful, for they will receive mercy;
the pure at heart, for they will see God;
the peacemakers, for they will be called the children
    of God;
those persecuted for righteousness' sake, for theirs is the
    kingdom of heaven.[2]

These blessings are referred to as the Beatitudes. To *beatify* means to make blissfully happy. The Beatitudes are verses that make you blissfully happy. Jesus is describing what life will be like in the kingdom of heaven[3] and telling people what awaits them if they have faith and live in a way that makes them ever ready to receive it. If you live in this way, it doesn't matter if

---

2 Matthew 5:1–12 (abridged).

3 Matthew calls it the kingdom of heaven; Mark and Luke call it the kingdom of God.

you're poor, or sad, or having tough times, the kingdom will be there for you. For all who have lived according to their ideals of righteousness, mercy, purity, and peace, especially if they are persecuted for it, there will be corresponding rewards in the kingdom of heaven.

As you saw in the examples from Matthew back in chapter 5, Jesus speaks several times about the day when the Son of Man will return to judge the world. Perhaps, therefore, the Beatitudes refer to this future time and the good that is in store for those who are mentioned in the verses. However, as you saw in the last chapter, the words of Jesus have practical spiritual value for you now. Regardless of any future judgment, good or bad, the life you lead now is what determines who you are.

The one key message that virtually all schools of Christian thought have agreed on is that through your faith in Jesus Christ and his messages—faith in God and his kingdom—you will one day know God and live in the kingdom.

Applying this key message of faith opens up possibilities for the spiritual understanding of these verses as they pertain to your life: If you don't know God or the kingdom yet—that is, if you are poor in the kingdom's wealth (poor in spirit)— by your faith and seeking you shall come to know it. If you mourn—if for a time you don't perceive God's presence or feel happiness—through your faith you will be comforted by Spirit. Those who hunger and thirst for righteousness (to be in harmony with God), through their faith, seeking, living righteously, and loving others will be filled with God's Spirit. There is a spiritual education going on here for you. The Beatitudes show you how to live in such a way that you will be filled with God's bliss.

These are sayings to which everyone can relate. The love of Jesus favors no rank or religious authority. Maybe this is why his sayings have taken such deep and lasting root in our culture. Everyone is equal in Jesus' eyes and all are called to be righteous.

What lies at the heart of righteousness, he says, is for your actions to be driven by virtue. "When you give to the poor do not tell anyone; do not let your left hand know what your right is doing."[1] He wants you to help people for the right reason—because you *want* to help them; not to gain approval.

"When you pray, do not do so in order to be seen by others."[2] "When you fast, do not look somber and visibly suffer such that others know you are fasting."[3] He wanted you to be genuine in all things, not to be doing the right things for the wrong reasons.

In Luke's parable of the good Samaritan, Jesus highlights the value of mercy while also defining its purity.[4] A man has been beaten and robbed and lies half dead at the side of the road. Note that Jesus says a priest saw him and passed him on the other side of the road. A Levite, a temple assistant of another Jewish tribe, also passed the man by. But the Samaritan, who was considered an outsider to the others, feels pity for the man, tends to his wounds, and takes care of him. It is this man whom Jesus prizes, because he is the one who showed mercy to another. Love and goodness are defined by one's actions and what is in one's heart; not by one's religious status.

---

1 Matthew 6:2–4.

2 Matthew 6:5.

3 Matthew 6:16.

4 Luke 10:29–37.

Your faith in God is one part of who you are; your actions are another. Neither is meant to negate the importance of the other. It does not devalue faith to say that good deeds are not dependent on faith. There is, however, a love that shines through these teachings that is not reliant on your beliefs about who Jesus is. The values Jesus outlines are based on the authenticity of your spiritual/social practices. Are you truly a righteous person; do you care for others; do you desire to live in a righteous world and stand up for what's right? This is not to imply that belief doesn't matter—in fact, your belief as pertains to salvation is the most repeated message in the Gospel of John. However, it is equally important to remember that the first three Gospels of the New Testament contain the majority of the words Jesus spoke. Their messages should at least not be slighted as less important than faith.

Jesus did not burden you in the Synoptic Gospels with complicated details about what you ought to believe theologically; he wanted you to know there is a kingdom of God, and love is the way to get there. "For my yoke is easy, and my burden is light."[1]

A good way to wrap up this short summary of the loving teachings found in the Synoptic Gospels is to look at Jesus' love of children. In his own words, "Let the little children come to me; do not stop them; for it is to such as these that the kingdom of heaven belongs. Truly I tell you, whoever

1 Matthew 11:30.

does not receive the kingdom of God as a little child will never enter it."[2]

It wasn't that Jesus valued children more than adults; rather his words indicate we should all strive to be humble, to maintain an open mind, and to have a joyous heart. It is the purity of the child that Jesus adores (relative to God we are all little ones at any age). This is another message that is important enough to have been mentioned a few times in each of these three Gospels. Were you ever lit up inside as you watched children laugh and play? "For it is to such as these that the kingdom of heaven belongs."[3]

There is no mention or intention in these words of Jesus' that our relationship with God should be governed by fear. At what age do you teach children that if they think the wrong thoughts they could be condemned to hell for all time? It seems a complex matter and a sinister concept for a child to bear. Are we as adults any more ripe for abuse?

The good news is, there is a kingdom and Jesus wants you to enter it. The Synoptic Gospels provide an instruction manual for the soul. They define the actions and values that will make you ready to do that.

Seeking

Among the first words out of Jesus' mouth in the Gospel of Mark is an exhortation to believe the good news: "The

---

2 Mark 10:14–15. This is similarly said in Luke 18:17 and Matthew 18:3.

3 Matthew 19:14.

kingdom of God is at hand."[1] What is the *kingdom of God* and what does *at hand* mean? Is the kingdom a place that will come into existence at the end of the world with the return of the Son of Man? Was it a place temporarily on the earth while Jesus lived? Is it a place you go to when you die? The kingdom can be interpreted to mean different things in different places in the Bible, and perhaps there is a lesson in that: the phrase "the kingdom of God is at hand" has deep-reaching spiritual implications that are like buried jewels waiting for you to dig and find.

Jesus provided a multitude of parables to help you in finding that understanding of the kingdom. A parable is a story that conveys a lesson or truth not found directly in the literal meaning of the words. For example, the parable of the good Samaritan discussed earlier in this chapter, or the one in the previous chapter about building a house on the solid foundation of Jesus' words instead of on sand. You can use these parables to assist you in gaining spiritual knowledge. But you must find the deeper meaning of these stories on your own. If you have the desire, reflecting on them can help you to find that meaning.

The kingdom of God is like:

seed sown on good soil, which bears fruit a hundredfold[2]
a mustard seed that grows and becomes the greatest of
    all shrubs[3]
a small amount of yeast that is mixed into flour and

---

1 Mark 1:15. This verse is also translated *the kingdom of God is near.*
2 Matthew 13:23; Mark 4:20; Luke 8:8.
3 Matthew 13:31–32; Mark 4:32–32; Luke 13:19.

leavens it[4]

treasure hidden in a field, which someone sells all
  he has to buy that field[5]

a pearl of great value, which a merchant sold all
  he had and bought it[6]

a net cast into the sea that caught fish of every kind;
  they kept the good but threw out the bad[7]

a bridegroom for whom virgins kept their lamps lit all
  night, not knowing when he would arrive[8]

a wedding banquet to which all are invited[9]

As was the case with the Sermon on the Mount, one view held throughout the ages has been that all of these metaphors found in the parables refer to the physical kingdom to come when the world is transformed with the return of the Son of Man. The kingdom being "at hand" meant it was due to arrive soon. Jesus preached in all three Synoptic Gospels that the kingdom would come within his current generation: "Truly I tell you, there are some standing here who will not taste death until they see that the kingdom of God has come with power."[10] Though, when it comes to scripture, again, it's possible that ideas are not as straight-forward or literal as they seem, and there are deeper meanings to be found.

Today, millions of people still believe that Jesus will return within their lifetime, bringing about the end of this world

---

(4) Mt 13:33; Luke 13:21; "leaven" means to make dough rise.
(5) Mt 13:44. (6) Mt 13:46. (7) Mt 13:47–48.
(8) Mt 25:1–13; similar saying Lk 12:36–40. (9) Mt 22:2–10.
(10) Mk 9:1; Mt 16:28; Lk 9:27.

as we know it. However, the most popular view today (among people who believe in a kingdom of God) is probably that the kingdom is a spiritual realm you will enter after you die. If you have accepted Jesus Christ as your Lord and Savior you will enter the literal kingdom of heaven.

My belief and experience is that we can begin to know this kingdom, this place of God, this realm of Spirit while we are on earth. (Going forward I will sometimes refer to this as the kingdom of Spirit.) Said another way, we can understand what Jesus meant by the kingdom by using our own spiritual experience and progression as a reference.

In the first parable listed above, Jesus speaks of the seed that fell on good soil and produced a hundredfold. He explains what this means in a later verse: "the seed is the word of God (or word of the kingdom)."[1] The good soil refers to those who "when they hear the word, hold it fast in an honest and good heart, and bear fruit with patient endurance."[2] In other words, you receive (read or hear) the words of God, and as you reflect on them and come to understand them, their wisdom transforms you for the better. The hundredfold crop produced is your spiritual bounty in a realm called the kingdom of God (the kingdom of Spirit).

In another verse, he compares the kingdom of God to a mustard seed that, when planted and tended, grows into the greatest shrub. This means when you harbor even the smallest seed of spiritual knowledge within you, you can, by giving it your attention and seeking, grow into an evolved spiritual being.

I believe we can see this parable's truth manifest before our

---

1 Luke 8:11; Matthew 13:19; respectively; Mark 4:15 "the word."
2 Luke 8:15; Mark 4:20; Matthew 13:23.

eyes in the Synoptic Gospels. When you read Mar¹
you find it is the most terse. As most Bible scholars ¹
(at least in my studies), Matthew and Luke acquᵤᵤᵤᵤ ᵤᵤᵤᵤᵤᵤ.
of their source material from Mark (which is why the three
Gospels are so similar and supports Mark as being the oldest
Gospel). Most of the verses I've mentioned so far, focusing
on love and how you should treat others, come from Matthew
and Luke, and are much embellished from the basicteachings
in Mark. For this reason, I can't help seeing the seed of the
kingdom in Mark's material as having blossomed in Matthew
and Luke. Perhaps we could continue to the let the kingdom
blossom in the understandings we have today, and in generations to come.

In another parable, the kingdom is like a net cast into
the sea. Think of all the books you've read in your life, or
all the spiritual teachers you've heard speak, as the sea into
which you cast your net. The "good fish" are the messages of
wisdom and truth you retain, which in turn transform you
for the better, the bad ones you throw back.

Or, think of yourself as a merchant seeking pearls. The
great pearl you find is your growth in spiritual understanding
and the expanding love you give, receive, and feel as a result,
which would be worth selling all you own to buy.

The many parables relate to the kingdom of Spirit in different ways, thus providing you with a variety of options to
assist your understanding. They are themselves good seed.
A parable is only mysterious if you don't understand what it
means. When you read something you don't understand, you
have a few choices. You can accept that you don't understand
it and turn away. You can ask someone to explain it to you

(although you might then understand the explanation without internalizing it, which means you might not benefit from it). Or you can think about what it means, search within, use your intuition, and figure it out. Seek the kingdom, ask for understanding, knock on the door because you want it to open.

As you start to better understand the kingdom through understanding one or more of Jesus' parables, metaphors, or other spiritual messages, you will find that it becomes easier for you to understand others. In Matthew (and similarly in Mark and Luke), when the disciples ask Jesus why he speaks to the people in parables, he answers, "To you it has been given to know the secrets of the kingdom of heaven, but to them it has not been given.[1] For to those who have, more will be given, and they will have an abundance; but from those who have nothing, even what they have will be taken away."[2] In other words, the understanding of Jesus' words will reap more of the same—an exponential growth in your understanding. No understanding, with no desire for understanding, will yield only less understanding.

The words of Jesus were meant to help you become a better person. Not only did he want you to love God and love other people, he wanted you to have an active spirituality and grow in understanding of it. Yet many of the religions that developed in his name over the centuries after he died, con-

---

1 Matthew 13:11; similarly said in Mark 4:11 and Luke 8:10.
2 Matthew 13:12; similarly said in Mark 4:25 and Luke 8:18.

tradicted his words and focused only on the command t
ship him. It's as if the great humility Jesus showed in tl.. ....
three Gospels—teaching you about love, God, your spiritual
potential, but rarely about his own divinity—was not taken
as sincere—as if he didn't really mean what he was saying
when likening you at all to himself in terms of your ideals and
spiritual potential. Believing in Jesus as your Lord and Savior
took precedence over all the other teachings in the Gospels—
leaving that material in a distant second position. At my
church, the second position material made for useful Sunday
sermons, which surely helped guide us in our lives, and are
the basis of Christian values, but it all amounted to not much,
relative to the fundamental requisite of belief.

A preacher might believe he is being humble and serving
the Bible because, he says, only Jesus knew God intimately,
and only through belief in Jesus could you get to God. (Let's
take as a given that the preacher is genuinely loving and doing
what he thinks is right to help you.) But how is it being
humble for any of us to ignore the majority of the words Jesus
spoke and base a belief system on no more than a few verses
from the Gospels? How, in the light of these three Gospels,
which embody such love, did we ever come to reduce
Jesus' teachings to a single dogmatic and fearsome ultimatum:
believe or burn?

For many years something gnawed at me—burned in me.
Something didn't feel right. God was being used, slighted,
misappropriated to serve the agendas of those who wanted
everyone else to accept what they believed about God and
their interpretations of scripture, without question.

Stepping aside for a moment from biblical interpretation,

based on what I knew of God from my own spiritual life, God did not threaten. God did not use fear as leverage to acquire souls. God did not reserve love only for those who believed a certain way, or thought the right thoughts, or said the right words.

Jesus seemed to want to fill me with love, while my religion seemed to want to drive my faith through fear. This was not an overt campaign of old-school fire and brimstone, and it's not that my religion didn't promote love (in fact, that is something I cherished about my religion, which drew me to it in the first place), and more and more I have noticed a shift toward staying focused on love in many denominations. But the threat of judgment and the exhortation to be prepared for the next world is always there, whether unspoken for an entire sermon or rarely mentioned by anyone outside of church, stoking an eternal fire of fear, which undermines love no matter how lovingly we dress it up or how lovingly we act.

There is a wonderful small book in the latter part of the New Testament called I John,[1] which seems to me to contain some messages that are among the most purely inspired by Jesus' messages:

God is love, and those who abide in love abide in God, and God abides in them. (1 John 4:16)

God is light and in him there is darkness at all. 1 John 1:5)

ere is no fear in love. (1 John 4:18)

---

ns First John, not to be confused with the Gospel of

Jesus seemed to want to empower me through love to find the kingdom of God, while my religion seemed to want submission. Having learned about the ego, I could sense it was up to its old tricks—making itself comfortable and safe. My preacher's ego, my ego, and the egos of those around me at church—all seemed to have the same agenda: don't question any of this stuff too much; accept what you are told. The collective fear made each of our own fears seem normal; together we accepted our place of separation from God. We all believed God made our religion, and who among us should question God?

This left a disconnect between Jesus' telling me to seek God, which meant asking questions, rather than simply accepting what I was told. Why was I being led away from searching for the answers?

The preacher taught that you are a separate being, but this is how you can feel comfortable as a separate being: "Accept Jesus Christ so you can go to heaven when you die and then be together with God." It's not that he was out to harm you or prevent your spiritual growth— his love was sincere. He was doing the best he could. But someone taught him, just as he taught you. His sermons were as much about helping himself to find peace as a separate being, as they were genuinely intended to help you.

A New Way to Discern God's Words

When it comes to the interpretation of what it says in the Bible, the debates can be endless. Perhaps a good way to determine which are truly the words of God would be to see how their results are or were manifested in the world. Would it be fair to say that if any of God's messages limited your spiritual growth, fulfillment, or happiness, it would be a good indication that the source of those words was not God, or that the words or their meaning got altered along the way from their origin to you? Or, if you were taught anything that prevented you from loving others—such as judging them for believing differently from you or imagining them to be condemned—would you agree that is different from what Jesus originally taught? Perhaps almost all of the spiritual words you've been taught were actually God's, but if men added or altered even a small number of them, their meaning could go astray. A pot of delicious soup can be ruined by adding even a pinch of the wrong spice.

If Jesus said you can know God and find the kingdom of God yourself, yet you are unsure if God is in your life or if you are living up to what's possible for you, hasn't something gone awry somewhere in what you've been taught?

If Jesus preached a ministry of love, but you are being given reason to fear, isn't something wrong?

Remember, your religion is a construct of men. Even if a man teaches you the Word of God, he is a man. He is imperfect. He is not the Word. He is not God. If he tells you ninety-nine things that are correct, that doesn't mean one thing he tells you can't be wrong. Be careful. You live in an ego-dominated world, and where ego and ideas about God interact, conflict is inevitable. What should you do if an ideological conflict occurs between you and your religion? Will you just ignore it—be afraid it could cause you eternal harm to question what you've been told?

You are taught that God's words are perfect, and if you have any trouble understanding them, or you disagree with any of them, or you find contradictions among the perfect words, it is because you are a mere imperfect person. You're told that if you can't find the truth of the words yourself it's okay—you must just accept what you're told they mean. This is another ruse of the ego. It's to the ego's advantage if you don't quite understand God's words and stay in your place, removed from the study and knowledge that would grant you firsthand authority in spiritual matters. A separate being, in separate understanding, looks for validation in being separate; your ego wants you to believe your place in this life is to remain separate from God and will try to support that position in any way it can.

If God wants you to find him, however, he could not mean for you to remain separate from him. He could not mean for you to fear him, or to fear questioning him, or to fear questioning anything. If God is love, he could not want you mired in the fear of condemnation. So now let's take a look at where most of this talk about condemnation comes from.

CHAPTER 8

THE GOSPEL OF JOHN

Unlike its three Synoptic predecessors, which discuss the importance of who you are and what you do as criteria for judgment, the Gospel of John focuses on your salvation being determined by belief. It also contains some of the most powerful verses interpreted to support the doctrine of fear, simply because they speak of judgment. Those interpretations, however, take great liberties with the actual words in the Bible, which could well mean something different from what you have been told.

The following is our fifth and, to my mind, most significant of the only eight verses in which you will see consequences directly related to not believing, because it is often cited to support the belief that you are damned to hell if you do not believe in Jesus as the only Son of God:

Whoever believes in him is not condemned, but
whoever does not believe stands condemned

already because he has not believed in the name
of God's one and only Son. (John 3:18)

What does "condemned" mean? The word itself means receiving a negative sentence or judgment. In this verse, believers can agree it is God's judgment. But does condemned, as it appears here, mean sentenced to hell, or is it referring to something else? It is most commonly understood as referring to hell, even though the word hell is not mentioned a single time in the Gospel of John.

This verse has three sister verses that say basically the same thing (the last of our eight verses) :

Whoever believes in the Son has eternal life, but
whoever rejects the Son will not see life, for God's
wrath remains upon him. (John 3:36)

I told you that you would die in your sins, for
you will die in your sins unless you believe that
I am he." (John 8:24)

The one who rejects me and does not receive my
word has a judge; on the last day the word that I
have spoken will serve as a judge. (John 12:48)

As John 3:18 is by far the most quoted of these four verses, and as they are commonly understood to have the same meaning, let's address them all by addressing John 3:18.

On its own, out of context, it's easy to deduce that you're damned to hell for not believing in Jesus. To make that meaning work, however, you have to look at the words isolated not only from what Jesus says in the three preceding Gospels (where hell is not once equated with not believing), but also from most of the other words in the Gospel of John.

To begin with:

> Your religion focuses intensely on your needing only to believe in Jesus. Yet Jesus did not point to himself as the principal object for your attention. Jesus spoke of all power coming to him from God.

Elsewhere in John, Jesus says:

> Very truly, I tell you, the Son can do nothing on his own, but only what he sees the Father doing; for whatever the Father does, the Son does likewise. (John 5:19)

> Do you not believe that I am in the Father and the Father is in me? The words that I say to you I do not speak on my own; but the Father who dwells in me does his works. (John 14:10)

Then Jesus cried aloud: "Whoever believes in me
believes not in me but in him who sent me."
(John 12:44)

I can do nothing on my own.
(John 5:30, abridged)

These messages are repeated several times in John.[1] So why
does the same Jesus who wants you to know that if you don't
believe in *him* you are condemned, also tell you that everything
he teaches and does comes from a higher authority? If Jesus
himself says the Son is nothing without the Father, why is it
taught that your eternal fate is dependent solely on your belief
in the Son?

This type of message is attested in the Synoptic Gospels
as well:

As he was setting out on a journey, a man ran
up and knelt before him, and asked him, "Good
Teacher, what must I do to inherit eternal life?"
Jesus said to him, "Why do you call me good?
No one is good but God alone."
(Mark 10:17–18)

But Jesus looked at them and said, "For mortals it
is impossible, but for God all things are possible."
(Matthew 19:26)

---

1 John 6:38, 7:28, 8:28, 12:49, 14:28.

That Jesus called your attention to God as the principal Source is not to say that he didn't also want you to be aware of his own spiritual identity. There is no message in John repeated more than Jesus telling you to believe in him for eternal life, and sometimes he tells you just to believe in his words.

I tell you the truth, he who believes has everlasting life. (John 6:47)

but those who drink of the water that I will give them will never be thirsty. The water that I will give will become in them a spring of water gushing up to eternal life. (John 4:14)

that everyone who believes in him may have eternal life. (John 3:15)

I am the light of the world. Whoever follows me will never walk in darkness but will have the light of life. (John 8:12)

I've counted twenty-four such statements in the Gospel of John. In very few instances, however, do these positive statements also mention a negative judgment or outcome if you don't believe. Why is it that we take the few verses threatening a negative judgment, such as John 3:18 or its three sister verses, and empower them to be as important as the other hundreds of other verses Jesus spoke in the Gospel combined?

Why must all positive statements about salvation be considered to imply the alternative possibility of condemnation, even when condemnation is not hinted at in the verse itself? Indeed, why must the entire good of Jesus' ministry—all the promises of salvation and all the teachings of ethics, values, and how to be a good person, which fill up most of the pages in the Gospels as to what Jesus said—only work if the greatest fear is invoked with it?

It's because the separate being sees a reflection of its own separation: You can't have eternal life without there being eternal death; you are either with God or without God; you are separate now, but you can be with God later; those who don't believe now will be separated for eternity. This is all separatist thinking.

The ego likes things simple; it likes yes or no answers—you either believe or you don't—the rest of the writings don't matter all that much. The idea that believing or not believing could lead to anything other than simple corresponding results (heaven or hell) does not compute for your ego—or so it would have you believe. But condemnation has a more involved meaning than you being sent to a place of eternal suffering.

Take another look at John 3:18:

> Whoever believes in him is not condemned, but
> whoever does not believe stands condemned
> already because he has not believed in the name
> of God's one and only Son. (John 3:18)

Jesus is speaking in the present tense. He does not refer to a future judgment and and say, "Those who believe in him *will not be* condemned." He says, "Those who believe in him *are not* condemned." He does not say, "Those who do not believe *will be* condemned." He says, "Those who do not believe are condemned *already*."

Said another way, if you do not believe in who the Son of God is on earth, you probably don't know God—don't have an interactive relationship with God—and that is its own condemnation. If, on the other hand, you do believe in the divinity of the Son of God on earth, and learn from his example and instruction that if you strive to know God you shall, then you also believe in your own relationship with God, and this keeps you from being condemned.

Jesus is telling you that your own relationship with God is what keeps you in the light. This one of the primary messages of all the Gospels. If you can't believe in God on earth—abide in him—learn from his teachings, you are in the dark—you are spiritually dead—separate from God. This is your current state, not what comes in the future. "I have come as a light unto the world, so that everyone who believes in me should not remain in the darkness."[1]

However you want to interpret John 3:18, by the words alone, stating that one is condemned for not believing in Jesus Christ is not the same as saying that one will go to hell for it. This is further clarified in the very next verse:

1 John 12:46.

> This is the verdict: Light has come into the
> world, but men loved darkness instead of
> light because their deeds were evil.
> (John 3:19)

This line doesn't get cited nearly as often because it detracts from the power held in the doctrine of fear. Jesus refers plainly here to a condemnation on earth, not after death. The judgment occurred *before* men were made aware of the light that is Jesus, not after. They were condemned already "because their deeds were evil;" they could not see the light because they loved darkness and so were condemned again when the light presented itself. They continued their cycle of darkness.

Jesus said in Matthew, "If your eye is unhealthy, your whole body will be full of darkness. If then the light in you is darkness, how great is the darkness!"[1] In other words, if you choose to be an evil person (thinking and acting in ways separate from God), evil is all you will be able to see (separation is all you will know). You will experience more evidence of the truth of evil, which in turn strengthens the reality of evil for you.

In Luke, Jesus tells you, "Do not condemn, and you will not be condemned."[2] On its own, in offering this way to avoid condemnation, the sentence contradicts the absolute idea of being condemned for not believing. Yet it meshes perfectly with John 3:19, which emphasizes that what you do defines who you are. If you condemn someone else, that

---

1 Matthew 6:23.
2 Luke 6:37.

is, judge them or treat them poorly, you are also condemned because you are choosing darkness. If you don't condemn others, neither will you be condemned.

Now look at the verse that precedes John 3:18-19. Here Jesus says:

> For God did not send his Son into the world to condemn the world, but to save the world through him. (John 3:17)

He is saying, "I'm not here to condemn you." So, why would he then turn around in the next verse and say, "But believe in me or you are condemned?" Taken literally, these two verses don't make sense together. They are spiritually profound, and it takes time and contemplation to understand them. Read the group of verses together in order to make sense of them yourself (better yet the whole chapter or Gospel). To quote the one line that condemns you without the context of the two verses that surround it, allows its meaning to be altered.

> For God did not send his Son into the world to condemn the world, but to save the world through him. Whoever believes in him is not condemned, but whoever does not believe stands condemned already because he has not believed in the name of God's one and only Son. This is the verdict: Light

has come into the world, but men loved darkness
instead of light because their deeds were evil.
(John 3:17–19)

If you believe that Jesus said all these words, using John
3:18 to threaten everyone who doesn't believe in Jesus doesn't
work. The only meaning that works in the context of all three
verses is that the condemnation he refers to is the present
earthly state of those who are unable to see who Jesus Christ
really is.

Now, it could be said that condemnation in life is
logically followed by condemnation after life, but if Jesus
meant you would go to hell, why would he be cryptic about
it? Why did Jesus not say, clearly and directly: "He who has
not believed in me shall be condemned to hell"? Or, "He who
has not believed in the only Son of God shall be condemned
to eternal hell after he dies"? Jesus did not say these words,
but long after he died men attached this meaning to the words
he did say. Who are you going to believe?

Please consider the issues raised here the next time someone
threatens you with this verse. It is too easy to take for granted that
what you are taught is in the Bible. Do the research for yourself.
The words are all sitting right there in black and white and red.

If you are going to stick to the literal meaning of condemnation, you still need to deal with the fact that, as we

discussed in the previous chapters, when Jesus speaks about a time for judgment, he is talking about the judgment day at the end of the world, not an afterlife. This is not one of the mysteries of the Bible you have to dig for; it is written throughout the New Testament.

In one of the verses cited at the beginning of this chapter Jesus says:

> The one who rejects me and does not receive my word has a judge; *on the last day* the word that I have spoken will serve as a judge.
> (John 12:48; emphasis added)

> This is indeed the will of my Father, that all who see the Son and believe in him may have eternal life; and I will raise them up *on the last day.*
> (John 6:40; emphasis added)

While the Synoptics and John may differ concerning what the criteria is for salvation, there is one thing all four Gospels can agree on: *the last day* is when the Son of Man returns to fulfill the prophecy of God's final judgment of humanity. You read about it in the previous chapters and it is repeated elsewhere in John.[1]

However, I hope you will now see that to relegate condemnation to mean you will be sent to a place where you will suffer eternal physical torment is to think only in the simplest,

---

1 John 6:39, 6:44, 6:54, 11:24.

literal terms. If the richness of Jesus' teachings is all boiled down to mean that for now you need only believe or don't believe, and later the judgment comes, your spiritual life in between is rendered inconsequential.

This type of thinking causes even Jesus to be thought about in over-simplified, two-dimensional terms—he is the Lord or he is not; his humanity is all but disregarded as unimportant. It is as important to understand who Jesus was, as he lived, in order to understand his teachings. One of the best avenues for this is to delve deeper into the other central component of John 3:18—the meaning of the Son of God. This is not such a simple matter either, much as we might like it to be for our ease of understanding.

The Son of God

The words Son of God are usually taken literally to mean that Jesus is the son of the Father (God). But the Son of God is also a spiritual term requiring spiritual understanding. The part of Jesus that we call the Son of God is his spiritual being. One way to look at the name Jesus Christ is to say that Jesus is the name of his human self, and Christ represents his spiritual being. Christ is the Son of God, living through the man Jesus.

The Son and the Father share the same spiritual nature. If you recognize one you recognize the other. "And whoever sees me sees him who sent me."[1] The term Son of God describes a relationship to God—the spirit within Jesus as it relates to the Spirit of God. It is the flame of a candle as it relates to a bonfire—the same substance, so to speak, to a lesser degree.

---

1 John 12:45.

While the Son and the Father are of the same spiritual essence, such that Jesus said, "The Father and I are one,"[2] he also knew there was a major distinction between the Son and the Father, "The Father is greater than I."[3] It is in the living example of his duality as both the Son of God and a man that Jesus teaches you to understand who you are, which is the only true path to discovering for yourself who the Son of God is.

Recognizing the Son is a subtle awakening. You cannot know the Son merely by worshipping the Son. You believe in the Son and thereby accept that the Son is real, but rather than believing that the Son of God is outside of you somewhere, perhaps heaven, you come to know who and what the Son is through knowledge of your own spiritual being—your soul, which shares the same nature with the Son. But like the Son to the Father, there is a distinction of degree in the relationship between you and Jesus Christ.

The word "realized" has long been used to refer to one who has been spiritually awakened—one who lives in conscious awareness of the truth of who she (or he) is—a spiritual being enrobed in flesh. This person has gained knowledge of God and actually lives according to spiritual lessons learned (that is, walks the walk); Spirit lives through this person, who talks and acts in godly manner. Such people have, for example, realized the wisdom of love—know how it feels and how it fulfills both them and those with whom the love is shared, and so express that in how they live and treat others each day.

To say the Son is a realized spiritual being means the spiritual being is awake in reality (real-ized); his or her light shines

2 John 10:30.
3 John 14:28.

in the world. Jesus said, "No one after lighting a lamp puts it under the bushel basket, but on the lampstand, and it gives light to all in the house."[1]

To recognize that Jesus Christ was the *fully realized* spiritual being on earth is to say he was the fully realized Son of God—the perfect Son—"God in the flesh"—shining perpetually—Spirit living fully in the world through a man. This is not some empty title of worship. It refers to something real and active—the living God.

Accept for the moment that Jesus did mean you were in the dark already (condemned presently) if you could not believe he was the Son of God. This means that if you can't accept the truth of a spiritual being who could be fully realized, you are also denying the god in yourself—the truth of who you are and your own potential. This keeps you from being realized in your truest, highest identity, which would lead to your most fulfilled life, and this ignorance of who you are might also lead to much suffering, as you make mistakes and don't know why, or even that you make them, and cause yourself or others pain, which could lead to your most unfulfilled life. This is the condemnation.

And further, if you can't believe in at least the possibility of who Jesus was, and you thereby deny the possibility of who you are, you are kept from knowing God as well as you could. For if you don't believe you share the same nature as God, you have no reason to look within yourself as a means to know God better and live in the realization of that knowledge—you are spiritually stifled. You cut yourself off from the spiritual

---

1 Matthew 5:15; parallel vs Mark 4:21; Luke 11:33. A bushel basket is an ordinary basket of the size needed to carry a measure of goods called a bushel.

life of God that flows through you. Therefore, when Jesus said you were condemned if you couldn't believe in the Son of God, he was also saying that you could not believe in yourself.

There are, however, many who would say that Jesus was not speaking in such general terms and he specifically meant that anyone who did not believe in him as the *only* Son of God would be condemned.

Jesus as the Only Son of God

The identity of Jesus Christ as the only Son of God is the core belief of all religions conceived in his name; he was the Messiah—the one and only—and it is only through his divinity that you can be saved. Do you agree this is the most important belief for you to have?

If so, isn't it odd that calling him the only Son of God is not mentioned in Matthew, Luke, or Mark, all of which speak of him as the Son of God but not as the only Son? John is the only one who repeatedly makes that distinction. He does this four times.

...as of a father's only Son... (John 1:14)
...It is God the only Son ... (John 1:18)
...he gave his one and only Son ... (John 3:16)
...in the name of God's one and only Son. (John 3:18)

Regardless of what you believe, endless debate, prejudice, hate, torture, and even killing have resulted from those words.

Throughout the ages and up to the present time, crusades, inquisitions, pogroms, and innumerable other systematic practices of harming, suppressing, ostracizing, seizing of property/possessions, stripping of rights have been perpetrated against people who held non-Christian beliefs. How did any church or nation ever end up with a creed in action of: "Accept the eternal loving light of the only Son or we'll kill you"?

If you look at the manifest results of biblical words as an important part of the criteria for determining whether or not they are God's words, something is wrong with the words of John above. If the above four verses are indeed God's words, then is it fair to say the words have been grossly misinterpreted? And if that is the case, shouldn't God's words have been formed in a way that would preclude the sort of misinterpretation that could lead to such atrocities? Think about the kind of man Jesus was when he lived, what his ministry was about, and decide if you think it could have been Jesus' will for people to be harmed in his name.

Very often these atrocities have been excused by saying that, at the time they were perpetrated, people didn't know any better. And surely there have been cases throughout history where perpetrators were ignorant and thought they were justified. It's more likely, however, that men did know better and used those exclusionary words as a religious justification for their actions against whomever they deemed to be enemies or whose interests were not in accordance with their own.

Your religion knows better now in that it does not physically harm those who don't believe.

> However, it still proclaims that the rest of t
> world's people who do not hold its same b
> are condemned. This is an issue your religion
> deems outside of its hands—regardless of the
> result in the world. The voice of your religion
> says, "It's not our fault that people[1] choose not
> to believe the truth of the one and only way.
> Let's focus on the good those words have done,
> continue to do, and all the people they have
> helped to save."

The words calling Jesus the only Son of God have indeed done much good in the world. The strength of the language has drawn countless good, caring people to God and Jesus. However, there is no degree of good that offsets the reality of the bad. While you need not dwell on the harms that have resulted throughout history from those particular "only" words, should you just ignore them? Is it possible there could be powerfully good meaning in those words, yet also something wrong with them? Could the perfect words of God result in the torture and death of millions ... or even a few?

If you agree that the words of God should not result in people's getting harmed, and you believe "Jesus is God's one and only Son" are, in fact, the words of God, then something must be wrong with any interpretation of those words that brings about the results listed earlier. Only a faulty source— words that are not God's or a misunderstanding of God's

---

1 About 70 percent of the planet's population—roughly five billion people—who are not Christians.

words—could produce such grievous harms; only a bad tree can produce bad fruit.

It's written, *A good tree cannot produce bad fruit.*

Can you think of any harm that has come from the words *love your neighbor?*

John 14:6

In the arena of philosophy, even the most religious-minded might engage in friendly debate about Jesus' being the one and only Son and what that might mean. There is, however, another verse in John stating more directly that Jesus is the only way to God. This statement has been used to render all debates obsolete.

> Jesus said to him, "I am the way, and the truth, and the life. No one comes to the Father except through me." (John 14:6)

This is perhaps the most boldly, authoritatively, and frequently cited verse of gospel. It is put forth as the single most definitive statement from God declaring that Jesus is the only way. End of discussion.

The verse does have immense spiritual value, which we will be discussing in a later chapter. For now, however, I want to point out that—as with the words "only Son of God," and the ultimatum to believe or else—if you believe "except through Jesus" are the words of God, something is wrong with any interpretation of the words that not only brings about the harms cited earlier but also deny you the freedom to question or to explore other possible avenues to God or understandings of God.

Part of the problem, I believe, is this verse has been taken out of context and interpreted as a self-contained truth. In fact, though, it is embedded in a chapter rich with discourse about Jesus, God, and the Holy Spirit. And the entire chapter is surrounded by others that contribute to the verse's meaning. The best way to substantiate the meaning of this verse (or any verse of scripture) is by placing it in the context of everything else that portion of scripture has to say.

In this chapter fourteen of John, Jesus emphatically wants you to know to believe in God. In doing so, you will come to recognize the Father in the Son and the Son in the Father. If you can believe in the Son you can believe in yourself and, as he said, you can do the works he did and even greater works, and the Son and Holy Spirit will always be with you.

Unfortunately, historically and to the present day, our tendency has been to isolate John 14:6 and quote it as a stand-alone pillar of Godly command. You can, for example, often see it quoted on a banner hanging off the railing at a football game, or on a boxer's trunks, or on a billboard on a highway. While everyone has the right to love what verses of scripture they may, the undeniable reality is that this tendency has irrationally amplified the words *except through me* and given this particular verse a significance beyond all others. The unfortunate result has been to make it seem that scripture has only one critically important thing to say. In addition, and perhaps more tragically, the acceptance of this verse as the only truth that matters has set people against one another rather than to drawing us together to love one another.[1]

It's a single verse that, for nearly two thousand years, has kept people from digging deeper into biblical meanings, as well as from looking to other sources of enlightenment. After all, what's the point of looking elsewhere if Jesus is the only way? What's the point of even reading the Bible if that is all you need to know? Like it or not, believing that's all you need to know has resulted in many millions of people who believe in Jesus but have no need or desire to read the Bible or think for themselves, because its much easier to simply accept what they've been told.

If we know that all of these exclusionary concepts have caused no end of fear, people's being actually harmed throughout history, and walls' being built to separate one group of believers from another, why is it so hard for us to explore what might be inaccurate about our interpretations of such words? What is it that keeps us dead set on interpreting everything in simplistic and literal terms, regardless of how the consequences play out in individuals or the world? The answer is plain to see: religion dictates specifically how the Bible's words are to be understood, no questions asked.

The Power of Religion

For the moment, let's talk about my Christian religion simply as "religion," in order to make some generalizations that any of our Christian religions might have in common.

Religion preaches in absolutes. You have to believe either

---

1 "I give you a new commandment, that you love one another." (John 13:34; 15:12; 15:17).

all of the words of its scripture or none of them. You can't pick apart scripture sentence by sentence.

When did God say this?

God didn't. Religion did. Inadvertently or not, it removed the need for you to think independently.

Religion tells you that its words are the perfect words of God. Then it tells you that to question those words is to question God.

It's a quick sleight of hand. Who said religion was God? Religion did.

Religion said God said religion is God. Did you catch that? Religion says that to deny religion is to deny God. Think about the logic.

God may be in any of man's religions, but only a man's ego declares that his particular religion is made solely by God. This way there's no need to question anything.

In its beginning, religion said God inspired its doctrines. Somewhere along the way, however, man's ego got in the way of his endeavoring to write down God's words. Religion had the words of Jesus, but religion is comprised of men, and putting together the scripture was a collaborative effort of men. These men had vastly more writings of other men and oral accounts to sort through in order to determine which of them were most likely to be the words of Jesus. This didn't happen in one sitting but over the decades after Jesus died, through intense debates and conflicts concerning all sorts of issues, from minor questions of diet to the most major questions of theological interpretation. It actually took centuries to arrive at consensus—a winning side—and consolidate all those writings and oral accounts into one collection of books that would be deemed as the authoritative canon 'til kingdom come.

When the work was finished, religion held it aloft as its inspired scripture. But over time, religion then shifted from talking about "God-inspired words" to "the words of God"—absolutely. The entire text collectively came to be regarded as perfect, "the Word of God." Religion went from man's inspired and noble efforts to transcribe God's words to declaring that the words went straight from God to the page, into one infallible book. At that point, religion departed from truth—departed from reality—and now, these many centuries later, you have been made to fear questioning it all.

God tells you to seek the truth for yourself. Religion tells you to accept its truth blindly.

God encourages your questions. Religion does not.

There's no denying how much the world has benefitted from the words, the works, and the spiritual force of Jesus Christ. Whether you have been saved, spiritually educated, guided, enlightened, or just enjoy Christmas, the goodness resulting from Jesus is apparent. The spiritual identity of Jesus has not been called into question here—only our understanding of his words.

Can we, with all genuine reverence, and without diminishing one cubit of Jesus' stature, extend our toe onto a new path of understanding? Can we discard the two-dimensional thinking that says to change the way we think is to negate or dishonor the past? Can we dare to suggest that our religions are not perfect?

In most areas of our development as a people, we move toward greater enlightenment and even mock the ignorance of our past. We once believed that the world was flat, that leeching was advanced medicine, and flying was for the birds. Yet, when it comes to religion, we maintain a death grip on our ancient beliefs as if we were wrapped around a pole a thousand feet off the ground to keep from falling.

Clinging to ancient beliefs is not simply a matter of faith; it's a matter of fear. It's fear of what will happen if you question God. It's fear of what happens when you die. These fears long preceded Jesus. People feared God from the moment they were able to formulate the idea of God.

Jesus emphasized the concept of a God to love and a God who loves us. If we had pursued this love exclusively, rather than creating new fear, we might by now have looked on fearing God the way we view ancient people who feared that a comet or an eclipse signaled the end of the world.

If ours is a God of love, and Jesus is his Son, why has there been, and why is there still, so much fear related to our beliefs in him, as well as negative judgment towards others with different beliefs?

Can we boldly turn our gaze toward the possibility that *something* might be wrong with the way we understand Jesus' teachings? Call Jesus perfect; I will not deny you. Can you admit we are not perfect?

Remember what you've read here: out of the 3,779 verses contained in the four Gospels, there are only four that directly state you will be condemned for not believing in Jesus as the only Son of God, and there are four others that say there will be a consequence of some sort if you don't believe in him. Mathematically, the entire doctrine of fear is supported by eight verses, which comprise 1/500th of the Gospels containing the words of Jesus. That's one fifth of one percent.

Astounding, isn't it? What we have allowed? Our fixation on a relatively small object in our spiritual field of vision has blocked the full grandness of the light—like the sun eclipsed by the moon.

You might believe that even one Bible verse threatening condemnation for not believing in Jesus as the only Son of God suffices as a truth to fear. Just make sure you research for yourself what the verse is saying or what it might mean, and don't do yourself the injustice of ignoring everything else Jesus had to say. For the sake of your own knowledge and well-being, study all you can about the words of Jesus, inside and outside the Bible; from other sources besides the ones you're used to every now and then. Allow yourself to consider the possibility that you can be saved without the implied threat of condemnation. And if you at least determine in your studies that the condemnation Jesus spoke of is not an afterlife hell, consider that condemnation is simply not salvation, and perhaps that is hell enough.

Most harms that have ever come, involving the name of Jesus, through the minds and hands of men, for almost two-thousand years, come down to a single cause. It has been in our midst all along—in your religion's belief and at the heart of what hasn't felt right to you for so long now.

It is the crux of one line that has kept you from seeking the truth for yourself, and let only your religion tell you what the truth is. For too long, one word has put the cap on that curious open space inside you—which yearns to learn and know.

There is one single word forged by your religion—by man's ego—which transformed the meaning of everything Jesus taught. In so doing, it transformed Jesus in the psyche of your religion. This one word, posing as a testimony of faith, has done more to put Jesus out of your reach than all the years of your religion have done to bring you to him.

Have you figured it out?

CHAPTER 9
ONLY

This chapter contains the heart of the original material that came through to me that day in my car. It is almost entirely a verbatim transcription (except for the introduction, which was added later). The original text, however, came streaming as a poem would, with no regard for introductory statements or explanations, and so, in order to make it flow properly, as prose must, I had to build a few bridges.

The voice grows more powerful here. It is more direct. As a reminder, when the text here says "you," it is referring to me and to my experiences. Yet, even as I heard it, I sensed that it was also talking through me to whomever else would be willing to listen.

You'll have read some of these messages in earlier chapters, the difference being that you will now be seeing them in their original form, uninterrupted, as they first came. I hope everything you've read up to this point will enhance your understanding of them.

And finally, I experienced this voice as a powerful, sustained impulse of messages, which I wrote down as quickly as I could. But I am just a flawed human being after all—not a perfect medium. Any time God's words came to me it was through the filter of my life's experience and my ego (strived though I have to transcend it), and often using my own detailed experiences and understandings to communicate. I believe this is how God speaks to all of us.

So where does this leave you in terms of trusting me or this source? Where it always should: to decide for yourself which are the words of God and which are not. There are no writings in the world that should be above scrutiny, whether they are in the Bible, written by your favorite trusted author, or the words you'll be reading here.

My words are not meant to dictate the truth in a forceful manner, but rather to provide an opportunity for you to learn through them. If you can accept that there is a Holy Spirit at work here, it's critical to the process that you be honest with yourself. For the moment, allow yourself the indulgence of believing it is I, God, who speaks to you.

Remember, "God" is just a word. You could just as well call me a guide, speaking through a man. How do you suppose I could reach you if not through a medium you were capable of understanding?

Please check the cloak of your religion at the door and travel these pages on your own divine spirit and love of God. Keep an open mind. Put aside preconceived notions concerning God. Try to reserve judgments if they rise.

If you can't accept this is God, then ask the God you know, "If there's anything in these pages that you would like me to take in, let me know."

When I say, "remember" something—I am offering you a lesson. You will notice my lessons are filled with love—as I am—and are not about fear. Be careful of those who teach you to fear— be wary of those lessons. Fear is man-made.

If you can accept this fundamental concept— that I am a God of love—that fear has no place in me—you will have a powerful tool for determining whether or not any particular words speak my truth.

Only Versus Love

Consider the sentences that form the pillars of your religion:

"Whoever believes in him is not condemned."
"No one comes to the Father except through me."

These two sentences are fused into the master belief of your religion:

Only through Jesus Christ can you be saved.

Do you believe both these statements to be perfectly true:

"Only through Jesus Christ can you be saved."
"God loves you."

Your religion has taught you that "only through Jesus" is the single belief you need to have about being saved. It has taught you that this belief and my love are one and the same.

When you say the words, "Only through Jesus Christ can you be saved," does any fear come up? Are you certain or uncertain? Does the question of certainty bring up fear?

Ask yourself, "What if Jesus is not the only way?" Or, "What will happen if I don't accept Jesus as my Savior?" Do either of these questions elicit fear in you?

What about the statement "God loves you"? Is it possible to summon fear when you hear those words?

Remember, you will feel me through love. Something is amiss if you feel fear.

Do you believe that I love you unconditionally? If so, how does that impact the significance of the word "only" in the statement, "Only through Jesus Christ can you be saved?"

My love for you is not dependent on what you do or do not know. I would not condemn my children for not knowing something any more than you would condemn your children for not knowing algebra in kindergarten.

Whether or not Jesus is the only way, I could never condemn you for not knowing that truth or not understanding it, because my doing that would interfere with your ability to determine whether or not it is true. You can be scared into believing something called the truth, but you can't be scared into knowing it is the truth. Why would I envelop the truth in so much fear that you could never reach it, leaving you no choice but to blindly accept it?

The truth waits eternally for you to find it, just as I do. My truth is love. My words are light. If you seek and find the truth while on the earth, your life will progress in grandeur. If you choose to never seek, however, you will not be judged, though you may experience a life that is unfulfilled in certain ways. If you don't seek the truth, you will be condemned to not know the truth—that's all—and the truth is grand.

The spiritual teachings of Jesus, and the love he manifested in the world, are there for your ben-efit—nothing else. There is no divine rod coming down in absolute judgment, deciding if your soul is saved or damned based on your acceptance or rejection of those teachings. There is no punishment associated with your relationship to me or to Jesus.

If you believe Jesus is my son, and you know I am love, then Jesus is love. You know in your heart that love is the domain of his teachings. Anything you are told that falls outside the domain of love—such as you will suffer eternal physical torment if you don't know or believe something—is the stuff of ego and the ignorance of men (their ignor-ance of love), who could only understand his teachings in the most literal terms.

If you must find God, and "there is only one way to find God," then that is a command. It leaves you no options. If you try any other way, you will not find God. If you believe that, you are likely to be afraid, and fear has no place in love.

But the fear of not finding God is nothing compared to the fear of what will happen to you in the afterlife if you don't hold the right beliefs. You've been told that if you don't believe in the one and only son, Jesus, you won't be saved.

What does it mean to be saved? According to your religion, saved means that your soul will go to heaven after you die—you'll be saved from going to hell. What could be more terrifying than eternity in hell?

Regardless of whether "only through Jesus" is right or wrong, please understand that I do not work through mechanisms of fear.

It might be argued that "only through Jesus" is a loving message, because it is telling souls something they need to know. But if the reason for this statement is based on love, why would any aspect of it elicit fear? The message could just as easily be delivered in a way that does not create fear: "Through Jesus Christ you can find God." Inserting the word "only" transforms the sentence into a fearful proposition.

Your religion rallied around your need for this only way to avoid hell as its ultimate cause. Surely there are better reasons than avoiding hell to seek God or Jesus. Is fear required in order to love God?

When you consider the Jesus you know in your heart instead of the religion in your head, do you believe that Jesus intended your spirituality to be governed by fear? Do you believe that the sum total of the Gospel he delivered was to teach you that by accepting him as the Lord you would be spared from hell?

The life, spirit, and lessons of Jesus can only be understood through your own seeking. They may be taught, told, or shown to your mind, ears, and eyes, but are learned only by your soul.

Seeking is driven by love, not fear. Love is the

way to the kingdom of heaven, and you know it. I designed you to know it. Trust your heart, more.

The Lockbox of Fear

When you take the word "only" out of the sentence and say, "Through Jesus Christ you can find God," you do not diminish the truth or take away from the divinity of Jesus Christ. So why does the word "only" need to be there?

Only *through* Jesus has been misinterpreted to mean only Jesus: only Jesus knew me personally; you can only worship Jesus; you can stop looking once you find Jesus and accept him as your Savior.

Finding God is what's important. Stressing the word "only" serves to ensure your worship of Jesus Christ as your Lord, while Jesus' wish for you to find God and evolve spiritually is too often ignored.

Remember: The words of Jesus are intended to bring you to God and the kingdom, *not to Jesus.*

He speaks often of his Father in heaven so that you may know the Father. He speaks of your finding the kingdom yourself. He guides you to find God through him. Not once, however, does Jesus tell you to seek *him.* Yet this is what your religion has primarily emphasized:

ONLY

that you find, accept, and worship Jesus.[1]

In the centuries following Jesus' death, there were great conflicts surrounding the question of whether Jesus was equal to God or made by God. Your religion is an offspring of a resolution made ages ago, that Jesus and God were one and the same. The differentiation between God and Jesus was swept away; the humanity of Jesus got taken away, as if to acknowledge his humanity would diminish his divinity.

Rather than bringing you closer to me, your religion became a system to perpetrate your separation: God is God, Jesus is Jesus, you are only you, and this is how God designed it. However, being lowly, sinful, and separated is just fine, because after you die you will be forgiven and dwell in paradise for all eternity as a result of your belief in who you were told Jesus is. This ideology has only increased the distance between us and caused you to believe that the love you feel for me is, in and of itself, having a relationship with me.

The egos of the men who founded your religion couldn't acknowledge the humble notion that it was their creation—their response to an awareness of God—because that would allow for

1 Only my religion's ideology was being objectively addressed here; there was no intention here or elsewhere to label religion as a villain, or the men responsible for it as such, or ignore the good that my religion and others have done in the world.

the possibility of error, in which case the religion itself might be called into question and their ego's security would be in jeopardy.

So they called your religion perfect—the creation of God. And to protect it (and themselves) even more, they further declared that to question it or look outside the religion for answers could condemn you to hell. Any doubts or questions you might have were likened to temptations of the devil.

Which seems more of a devil to you: the force that presents you with a God and a religion you can never question, or the force that invites you to question and seek the truth of God for yourself?

Jesus preached and practiced for you to do the latter.

Not being allowed to question grants your ego exactly what it desires—security in separation. Your ego knows that if you are fixated on the divinity of Jesus as God's one and only son, you will not be looking beyond what your religion teaches you because you could never aspire to be like Jesus or to know what he knew anyway.

Unfortunately, while the ego's position is secured, your soul is secured in a different way. "Only" [through Jesus] traps you in one specific belief. It is a lockbox of limitation for your soul. The lockbox keeps the truth inside it and your seeking mind locked out. It's a manmade device that uses the fear of condemnation to protect your ego by preventing you from asking any questions. You've been told what is the "only" way, so you don't have to think, or seek, or find. Simply accept it or not; be saved or perish.

"Why is this truth so?" you ask your father.
"Cause I said so—that's why," he replies.

The founders of your religion came up with their fixed set of beliefs concerning Jesus, locked them in the box, and called them the holy words—not to be questioned—for all time. Paradoxically, if you open the box to examine the contents, you're in faithless violation; if you accept what you've been told as the truth, you can never *know* the contents. Seek by questioning the truth of the words "only through Jesus" and you are condemned for your lack of faith; accept the truth blindly, and you never get to find out if it's true. Just keep the sacred lockbox on a pedestal and look on with faith that you shall be saved accordingly when the time comes.

I invite you, in love-filled anticipation, to question me, and to grow and learn from me. You naturally have questions and maybe some doubts. This is honest. Yet you allow yourself to believe that uncertainty, curiosity, and an open mind are gateways to hell, and thus, you believe

that honesty is damnation. Isn't that silly? Do
you believe I could ever condemn you for being
honest? Would I, the loving God you believe in,
cast you into hell because heaven forbids you to
harbor any doubts?

You believe Jesus spoke the words "seek and
you shall find," and you believe they are my words,
but do you seek? Or do you simply accept what
religion has taught you and not trouble yourself
to seek?

Your ego knows you well. It knows what tools
are at its disposal. Everything surrounding the
word "God" is draped in holiness. Being caught
up in worship keeps you from seeking, and then
you're not doing what Jesus preached for you
to do.

Not thinking or questioning may be your
religion's commandments, but they are not mine.
You are told to believe in the Gospels, but nowhere in the Gospels does it tell you to blindly
believe everything religion tells you is the truth.
There's a critical difference between the words of
scripture and the interpretation of those words.
Just because the Gospel exists doesn't mean how
others have interpreted it is the Gospel too. And
even if your religion has interpreted all the words
correctly, you still need to come to understanding
on your own, if you are to benefit from them.

The only value of blind faith is that if you allow

yourself to believe in something, you might then be inspired to gain further spiritual understanding. If your faith entails a dark side born of what will happen to you if you don't believe, fear must be your copilot. Faith marred by fear thwarts your path forward. You will be tense, close-minded, and apprehensive about learning truth for yourself, because religion commands you to accept its truth as my own.

Blind Faith

Blind faith, you have been told, is of divine value. This rule works well for the separate being who is seeking comfort in being separate because it provides the only answer you'll ever need and prevents you from the discomfort of asking questions you don't know the answer to.

Imagine yourself as a computer that links to the spiritual-world-wide-web via a USB cable. What might harm the computer is a USB cable left disconnected and uncovered, leaving it prone to dust, liquid, or other corrosives. You can either plug the USB into Spirit—downloading spiritual information as quickly as your drive allows—or you can simply put a plastic cap on the end of the cable.

Blind faith is the potential of the cable with a cap on the end. In itself, it holds no value and earns nothing for your soul. The only value it has is your belief in me, which can and should inspire you to seek me—to plug into me—and keep on finding me.

The blind faith your religion prescribes is harmful because it tells you that you will gain entrance to heaven where you'll be with me after you die and causes you to not see the potential of your relationship with me right now—on the earth.

Will believing in Jesus decide the fate of your soul? Have you sought this answer from Jesus? He left plenty of material behind for you to study. Have you examined his words? Has it occurred to you that you have the ability to find the answer for yourself? You don't have to simply accept what you are told.

I gave you a great tool for progressing spiritually and evolving as a being—your mind. Blind faith tells you that you need not rely on your mind to answer the bigger questions or determine higher truths because Jesus did all the work for you. How convenient. Your religion, which was created after Jesus died, wanted you to accept all the answers it gave as coming from Jesus. It declared them by self-appointed divine authority. It warned you of grave peril for your soul should you think too much and corrupt the integrity of your faith.

I gave you your mind not so you should fear it, but so you'd use it to help you. What kind of God do you take me for, that I would give you the gift and power to think and then condemn you for doing so?

This, according to his words in the New Testament, is not what Jesus wanted. He wanted you to come to know God personally. Why would Jesus implore you to ask if he had already given you all the answers? Why seek, if they are already found? You are taught that Jesus is the ultimate role model, but then you are told to ignore some of what he said.

He taught you to love and believe and not to fear. He taught you the kingdom of God is yours to find, and you could find it on your own. Jesus advocated a genuine relationship with God over a religious practice that simply went through the motions or impaired people's path to finding God.

Now, two thousand years later, the tables have turned, and once again an old guard of bold men have declared what you ought to believe based on their own egotistical beliefs—our way or no way, believe or else.

Beware these heralders of fear, gloom, and doom. Lost are the ones who believe I command in absolutes. They are dragging you down to *their* self-created misery. It is they who fear their own lack of certainty—their own lack of firsthand knowledge.

They are afraid to think for themselves because they fear me. While they profess me to be a

merciful God of love, privately they believe I
am an unyielding, jealous, and judgmental God
who will cast them out as faithless for having the
temerity to think. Why? Because this is what they
too were taught throughout their lives, and what
they now, in turn, teach to you, usually with the
best of intentions.

It's humorous because they are aware of their
limitations, and yet they are still sure they know the
answers when it comes to God, creation, and death.

It's sad because, if you believe that only Jesus
could know me personally (only he was my son),
and the best you can do is to worship Jesus in
order to reach me after you die, you transform
yourself from a beautiful being of unlimited
potential into a limited being prone to a lifetime
of stunted growth.

Jesus taught you to follow in his footsteps; he
taught that you could achieve what he achieved.
Yet you are taught that the truth is: your only
spiritual goal should be to accept Jesus Christ as
your Lord and Savior.

Truth

What is truth? Men have fought and killed
each other for thousands of years because they
disagreed on what the truth is—who God is, what
God is called, what system of belief is right, and

which others are therefore wrong. It's like fighting over what love is—no fight is more foolish, more futile, or more tragic.

Many with absolute faith believe that Jesus spoke the truth with divine authority when he stated, "No one comes to the Father except through me." Belief, however, is different from fact.

The authority of the words "only through Jesus," and what they mean, has been passed down through untold generations to your religion today. And those who are in charge of your religion believe they are commanded by me to accept those words, as well as what they agree those words mean. Then they say these are God's words, rather than say they *believe* these are God's words. The meaning is defined as God's truth, and you are commanded to accept it.

Remember: I am not commanding you to accept *any* truth.

I present to you the truth. You may perceive the truth that sits before you or you may feel something to be true. However, there is no sentence presented to you that you can *know* as the truth before going through the internal process of mind that brings you to that truth. You can't be commanded to know the truth. If you are, it's never actually the truth you accept. It's only an image of something called the truth.

When you were younger and learned your

multiplication tables, you could memorize all the answers and be able to recite them at any time; for example, two times two equals four. But only when you process what that means, and realize if you lay down two sticks, then two more next to them, two sticks two times gives you four sticks, do you truly understand multiplication.

Likewise, you could memorize every word that Jesus said in the Bible, but spiritual truth is what you come to know through your own heart and mind—through me—and this knowledge transforms you. Your search for this truth is your own path. Your path should be one of inspiring revelations, not conflict. Your spirituality is not supposed to take you to a dark, frightening place with terrible consequences for your soul.

I love you so. I wish you knew the unconditional nature of that love. The tyranny of fear that is draped over your soul is absurd. It's absurd to know I love you and yet believe I would condemn you to eternal torment if you didn't happen to believe the right beliefs.

For many people, belief is based on whatever religion they happen to have been born into. Do you suppose my love is reserved only for those who happened to be raised in a Christian home? What about those who never heard of Jesus Christ? Do you truly believe I condemn them to hell based on the circumstance of their life? Do you think if you were raised in a Muslim home, in a Muslim land, you would hold the same beliefs you do now?

Salvation of the soul has devolved into the basic matter of whether you will go to heaven or hell after you die. Why worry about matters beyond your comprehension? Even the Bible does not give details of what happens when you die.

You don't have to pretend to understand that which you do not. You need only be genuine. There are many answers you can't know while on the earth; humility need not be contrived. It occurs naturally as a result of learning the truth, which is that you know so close to nothing, it can be said you know nothing at all.

The most difficult questions you can ask have been, and still are, unanswerable.

Was humanity created on purpose? Who or what is God?

Your ego deludes you into believing you have the answers. It deludes you into believing you need to know those answers. Its job is to make you feel secure in order to make itself secure.

Will believing in Jesus decide the fate of your soul?

Must your belief supersede your desire to seek such answers yourself?

Remember: I do not tell you *this* or *that* is

the truth. It is you who decides what the truth is. Don't let anyone tell you what the truth is. Don't let anyone tell you what God's words are. Let words be spoken or displayed to you, but seek within yourself to determine their validity.

Do you think Jesus has an ego requiring you to declare your blind allegiance to him alone, cutting off all other paths of learning?

[*But it is written*, I finally replied in thought.]

It is Written

Pang goes the fear again, eh? How you have loved absolute statements like "It is written." These words have granted you everlasting security. No more thinking. No more seeking. Just peace and comfort in the written words of God—answering all questions—laying down all laws.

What does "it is written" mean? It is written in the Bible—the one and only text you have to guide your life. It is often taught that I wrote every word in the Bible. But such an absolute statement is yet another manifestation of the paradox we've been discussing. You can't examine or question the words of God, which means you can't determine for yourself if they are true. The lockbox is not open for discussion. However, if you allow your religion to dictate what is true

instead of finding it for yourself, your religion—
not Jesus—becomes the steward of your soul.

The men responsible for your religion have you
so caught up in the absolute notion that its words
are God's words, you are prevented from looking
into the origins of those words. With ultimate fear
on the one hand and God's love on the other, they
have kept you in spiritual subservience.

I tell you, however, there is an endless amount
to be learned from studying the history of the
Bible's words, as well as in discovering for yourself what those words mean independent of that
history. How ironic that I should welcome your
open mind with love as the path to finding me,
while these others, claiming to shepherd your
soul in my name, preach that you should deny
your open mind because it will lead you away
from me. They have converted your spirituality
into a win or lose scenario.

The truth being kept from you is that you
don't need to subscribe to their paradigm. While
you are busy worrying about the two choices
presented to you, you fail to understand that it
was the men who created your religion, not I,
who have put that choice to you.

Accept their win or lose scenario and you are
caught in their paradox—you can't seek because
you have to blindly believe; but if you blindly
believe you can't get to know me. Your soul is

captured. The more of you captured, the safer *they* are. The more believers there are, the more validated are their beliefs.

It is written: "No one comes to the Father except through me."

Did I write that sentence? As they tell it, Jesus said this as me incarnate, and it is written in my book, so they are my words.

The authority of the Bible as a whole, and the meaning of the words therein is the same issue as the others we have been discussing whose roots and legitimacy must remain stuff of belief and cannot be called fact.

Is "only through me" a true statement? Is every statement in the Bible true? Is every word in the Bible written by God? These are all the same question.

The words in the Bible, of themselves, hold no spiritual meaning. All meaning lies in what you ascribe to them.

These are good questions. They can lead to knowledge.

The answers do not matter, because they don't affect the value of the written words. Your Bible has messages of truth and wisdom for you to find. But the value of those messages is to be found in the words themselves, regardless of who wrote them, even if you believe that author to be me. It is only the fear of damnation that has caused you to think otherwise.

Words are just words. Knowing who wrote the words doesn't change their meaning—for better or worse. If Joe Magillacutti wrote the words "Love your enemies," does that diminish their value?

For too long my name has been used to keep people from having to actually understand the words they so vehemently defend. "God spoke—accept and obey" is the creed of too many religions. Caught up in the argument over which words are God's, you are tempted to forget the primary importance of coming to understand the words themselves. If you truly believe all the words in your Bible are mine, shouldn't you then have the desire to study them earnestly?

Why must it always be an all or nothing choice? Why do you have to believe God wrote every word in your Bible or none of them? The answers to those questions are not beyond your comprehension.

My words are in your Bible. If you continue to seek, you will come to know which ones they are. Man's words are also in the Bible. All you need to know is that man had a hand in writing your Bible—even if only as an inspired scribe—in order to know that it likely contains flaws. Anything involving man's hand warrants examination—not blind acceptance.

If you heard Jesus speak, you could accept his Gospel directly. But the fact is, men were responsible for getting that Gospel to you. They were inspired, yes, but the Gospels you read are successive iterations, branched from the original source.

No one on earth can state with certainty what words Jesus exactly said and what their precise meaning was in every case. Even the closest translations can still miss the nuances or subtleties of the original language. This is why the meaning you glean from the words is more important than the words themselves. The words are not holy. Only your interpretation of them is.

You were told "only through Jesus;" told that the Bible is my book; told that all of its words are mine; told that if you question any of the words or their validity, you are lacking in faith. If you're lacking in faith, you're told, it's a short step to damnation. Damned if you open the box; in the dark if you don't.

If I love you, how could I damn you?

I damn you because I love you? It would be silly if so many people didn't believe it. The truth is yours to decide. It's yours to seek and find. You decide which words are mine.

You will not be saved solely because of what you believe. You will not be saved because you know one or more particular truths. You will not be saved because you believed blindly that I wrote every word in the Bible. You will not be damned because you didn't.

Believing Jesus to be the only Son of God, the Lord and Savior, the Messiah, will not, in and of itself, save you. Nor will not believing, in and of itself, condemn you.

Please now, stop.

Take a deep breath.

Know this, remember this:

You Are Already Saved

PART III

CHAPTER 10

SALVATION

Get on with the love. Get on with the seeking.

According to my religion, my soul is in danger; I need Jesus Christ to save me from hell and grant me eternal life in heaven. The words of Jesus, however, present a far richer and more profound meaning.

If needing to be saved means your soul is lacking something fundamental that it requires for salvation, you are already saved. If being saved to you means simply getting to heaven and spared from hell, you are already saved. You may be so caught up in the fear of what to do or believe in order to be saved, it doesn't occur to you that you don't need to be saved in these ways.

A thousand years ago, you might have believed that if you got in a boat and sailed to the horizon, you would fall off the edge of the world, and this would have been normal to believe. If you were condemned and put on a boat to sail straight to your death, chances are that when you were far enough from shore not to be seen, you would dive off the boat and swim for your life. You'd do anything to save yourself. You'd rather take your chances with the sharks than sail off the end of the world. Fear would prevent you from realizing there might be another possibility: there is no edge of the world.

It's the same with the belief that your soul needs to be saved from going to hell after you die—that life on earth is a believe-or-burn ultimatum of extremes and the meaning of your spiritual life is nothing more than accepting Jesus Christ as your Savior in order to get to heaven. This fearful belief system began in ancient times. It doesn't mean you have to keep believing it today.

You are a beautiful soul who already has everything you need for salvation. Don't let anyone tell you otherwise. If you believe you are incomplete or not good enough, you will fear that you won't be able to acquire what you need to be complete. How much greater then is the fear that you will not acquire what you need to get to heaven?

Don't ignore the hell that comes to mind and how it makes you feel when you imagine the afterlife consequences of not being saved. Your faith in Jesus Christ does not demand that you accept all the beliefs men have linked to his name. Whether based on a desire for control or the most loving intention to save you, the ancient need for you to be saved is filled with fear. If you need to be saved from something, there's something to fear.

Do you believe Christ is love? Proceeding from this assumption, the words of Jesus are there for your illumination, not to make you afraid. His words are good seed, not seeds of fear. He preached a ministry of love and your limitless capability to know God. Jesus had a larger agenda than saving you for the next round. And though he preached for you to believe in him, he did not ever talk about your inherent lack as a human being.

When Jesus says, "The kingdom of heaven is like treasure hidden in a field,"[1] does he follow that with, "but you don't have what it takes to find it?" When he says, "Ask and it will be given to you; seek and you will find,"[2] does he say that you are not fully equipped to follow this teaching?

If you were missing something you needed in order to find the kingdom of God, it would have been terribly remiss of Jesus not to tell you that. Instead, he says you must come to the kingdom as children, not as adults who know all the answers, or you will never enter.[3]

If Christ is love, then your pursuit of spiritual understanding and growth in his name should be about nothing but love. In love, there is no room or reason for you to fear that the details of your belief may not be exactly right or to worry about whether your understandings of scripture are correct. God wants you to learn and grow spiritually. Do you really imagine that your Creator, who knows your imperfection, makes a final judgment of you based on your knowledge or belief while you are still on your path to finding the answers? Or that you, in your imperfection, could do something wrong that God would never forgive?

Accept that you are loved unconditionally—not as some nice saying, but truly. Next time you look in a mirror of judgment, imagine that your seven-year-old child spilled a glass of milk. Would that cause you to declare you will never

---

1 Matthew 13:44.
2 Matthew 7:7; Luke 11:9.
3 Paraphrasing Matthew 18:3; Mark 10:15; Luke 18:17.

forgive her? Can you imagine your child doing anything that would cause you to withdraw your love? On the contrary, you would no doubt take on the world to defend her innocence, maybe even in light of a true crime. Do you imagine God loves you less?

The Forgiveness of Sin

Many words in the lexicon of spirituality have, over the ages, gathered negative connotations. One of these is "sin." You are told that your belief in Jesus Christ is the most important criterion for salvation, but, at the same time, sin is evoked as a barrier to being saved. Such a serious word sin is—laden with judgment—drenched in religious significance. You've heard throughout your life that Jesus died for your sins. It doesn't get more serious than that. Not only does this view of sin cast dark clouds over your perception of God's love, but it also can allow you to miss the practical understanding of sin that would benefit your life.

As we discussed back in chapter 6, sin is usually taken literally to mean a wrongful act—something we do to harm ourselves or others. The harm could be minor and easily fixed, or deeply scarring and doing permanent damage.[1] We then go a step further to say that sin is a transgression against God for which we are judged. However, we also discussed a spiritual definition of sin, underlying the literal. Death is the state of separation from God and sin is the act that puts you there. Put

---

1 To Jesus just a thought could be a sin—thinking in a way that is not righteous. He said, "Everyone who looks at a woman with lust has already committed adultery with her in his heart." (Matthew 5:28)

another way, sin is anything that separates you from your highest self.

Let's say, for example, you choose to drink a lot of alcohol on a daily basis. You are then choosing to live a somewhat blurred existence. While it may not be impossible to find God (or live in harmony with your idea of righteousness), your mind and emotions, which act as your guides, will be impaired. Drinking becomes a sin when you are no longer able to find God. Or, you could just say that drinking becomes a sin when you are no longer able to live the life you want and be happy. You are also damaging your body, which can have its own repercussions. Maybe your drinking goes a step further and starts to hurt other people in your life. Understanding why your actions (or inactions) led to any kind suffering can make sin, in and of itself, a great practical teacher.

Adding God's judgment does not give you the same kind of constructive feedback—perhaps you will do the right thing because you feel you have to, but the reason why you do it is not personally tangible enough. The purest reason to change sinful behavior is to benefit yourself or others. And isn't that doing it for God, anyway?

Perhaps you'd agree, however, that drinking too much, even with all the harm that may result, is a relatively minor sin, because you can still make a better choice, change your actions, and fix your situation. But what about the more damaging, grievous sins?

Leaving aside issues such as murder or sexual assault, let's say someone cheats on their spouse. Perhaps their marriage ends and the lives of both people, as well as their children (if they have any), are adversely affected in long term, important ways. Or what if while driving someone looks down at their phone when a message comes in and causes an accident that kills someone. In such a situation, the damage can never be reversed—someone lost their life, and there is also the collateral damage to all the loved ones connected to both parties.

If we look at just the sinner here in these cases, the permanence of outcomes resulting from his (or her) actions might create all manner of psychological trauma and suffering (unless, of course, he is a psychopath who doesn't care). However, in one sense, the results of major sins are the same as those of minor ones: existing in the state of being cut off from God or from our best selves—that is, spiritual death. In these cases, though, that state might seem exponentially harder to get out of. It is at any point of feeling disconnected due to our actions that we can most fear losing God's love.[1]

The question is whether the state of spiritual death is actually dictated by God, or is it something we create for ourselves? We do enough damage to ourselves through sin without bringing Godly judgment into the equation. We might feel emotional pain, regret, remorse, or guilt as a result of sinful actions, or we might have psychological battles to face, but these can also be valuable indicators of right and wrong, or of what is good or bad for ourselves and others.

Whatever sins or causes you could ever have, the deeper suffering occurs in your soul when you choose to believe that God's love is withdrawn from you. Or, put another way, you choose to believe you don't deserve love—you don't deserve to feel good or be happy, and then you are in darkness. That kind of spiraling self-torture can go on indefinitely as pain begets the pain of being in pain, and so on.

---

1 This is just one particular way to express this; one might not think of or even believe in God, yet have the same type of inner fear.

In my experience, the more clarity I've had, or the closer I am to God, the more painful it's been when I blow it, lose that clarity, and simply can't find God in the darkness. I can't find my highest thinking and best self, which I've been used to experiencing. Or when for reasons of life circumstances or relationships gone wrong I became depressed, I've wondered if I'd ever be truly happy again. But any time I've ever felt that way, through my perseverance and desire to overcome (and sometimes, I believe, with the guidance of Spirit) I was able to retrace my steps to find out where I went wrong and figure out what I could have done wiser. In doing so, I learned that my suffering was self-inflicted, not a punishment from God, and the suffering then became a great teacher as to how to avoid repeating it in the future. Many times, I realized that in my sadness I was in essence asking God, "Why have you forsaken me?" And I would find God staring back, saying, "Why have *you* forsaken *me?*" God's love is never withdrawn.

Rather it is we who choose to pull away from the consciousness of God, or said another way, from our clarity. It is we who choose what to think, and that choice is one of the few things in life we can control. We can then redirect our thoughts and take different actions; we can change our ways (repent). But as for Godly judgment or condemnation, if that is not our creation, you've certainly read enough now about the Bible's possible timing for that judgment. God's love, however, is shown by the more immediate solution to the problem of sin offered in the Bible.

It is written that when Jesus healed people, he often said, "Your sins are forgiven." The word sins, in this context, refers to the totality of your perceived separation from God. Although illness happens in the physical body due to physical causes, the perceived separation from God (spiritual death) is a metaphysical impediment to his ultimate healing force.[1]

Separation from God is how Jesus perceived sickness; this is what sickness was, relative to the fully realized spirit of Jesus. When he took the hand of the mortally ill and said, "Rise now," he infused them with the light of his truth: *There is nothing here but my divine presence; awaken to the truth of it within you and be separate from God no more; the perceived separation of sickness cannot exist in you.* Their sins were forgiven—wiped away like a debt would be forgiven—clearing the way for them to rise out of spiritual death, cleansed and reborn in the light of God.

Isn't this concept supposed to have been applied to all the world in the sacrifice of his life? If Jesus died to pay for the sins of the world, then the sins of the world—past, present, and future—were forgiven. So, are your sins forgiven, or aren't they? It can't be both. Even though you may believe you could transgress against God and thereby incur his wrath, if what it says in the Bible is true, you are already forgiven.

---

1 One last reminder: God is a name, a term, one way of denoting something. You could as well say, "the perceived separation from Spirit is an impediment to its ultimate healing force." The same truths can be expressed in different language. Invoking one's will, coupled with health and life-style changes and cleansing of one's body, are as much "finding God" and allowing healing forces to flow, as concerns healing. Let's disempower the language we use to be less important than the meaning we are after. The message is all that counts; the names, words, language, or context is not sacrosanct ever.

But of course there is an obvious catch: you must accept Jesus Christ as your Lord in order to receive this forgiveness.

Let's accept as true that the sins of the world were forgiven through Jesus Christ. If the world were that mortally ill person, then Jesus infused it with the light of his truth. The world has been shown that the darkness of separation is an illusion. Do you believe Jesus' forgiveness requires your faith in order to be activated? Is the world actually dark until you believe it is light?

If Jesus did what is said of him, the world was left in a state of forgiveness, a state of grace, a state of love. Sin is turning away from that state. You may have been taught that you were born a sinner and, as you inevitably act according to your nature, you must ask for forgiveness in order to regain God's grace. Now, instead of viewing yourself as a sinner, consider that you are a beautiful soul—a child of God—who occasionally acts against your nature and sins. Rather than reaching down from heaven and pardoning you because you have asked, God would only remind you of the eternal state of forgiveness you live in. In that reminder, your Father says, "Now sin no more."

As you choose love you are deciding you don't want to live in separation from God any longer and you recognize that your sins are already forgiven. You don't want to harm yourself or others, and you forgive yourself for the temporary ignorance that caused you to think or behave in separate ways.

This is one way to understand salvation—as the forgiveness of sin. It is the understanding that God loves you unconditionally. It doesn't mean it's okay to sin. It doesn't mean the wicked do not need to face justice in a real-world way or have a spiritual reckoning and repentance to make, for their well-being or other's. It doesn't mean you shouldn't acknowledge any wrong you've done or mistakes you've made and change for the better.[1] It means that no matter what you do, you are loved and the slate is clean. God will always welcome you with open arms. God's forgiveness is eternal.

This is precisely what is meant by, "You are already saved."

Being Saved

For God did not send his Son into the world
to condemn the world, but to save the world
through him. (John 3:17)

For I did not come to judge the world, but to
save the world. (John 12:47)

Accordingly, Jesus is called the *Savior* of humanity. What did Jesus mean by, "I came to save the world?" Did he finish the job? Are you saved?

You've been taught that you are not saved—or at least not born saved. Perhaps being baptized as a baby gives you that something. Or perhaps it is when you make a mature, conscious decision to accept God as central in your life. Most believers, however, can probably agree that you are the missing link in Jesus' completion of the job. You must accept Jesus Christ as your Savior in order to be saved.

This understanding of salvation comes from the perspec-

---

1 This is repentance—not for God's sake but for the right reasons—caring for yourself and others.

tive of separation. It tells you that you are separate from God, but then tells you how you can be with him someday. The perspective first creates your need to be saved and then tells you what to believe in order to be saved.

As it is written in another one of the most quoted verses from the Gospel of John:

> For God so loved the world that he gave his one and only Son, that whoever believes in him shall not perish but have eternal life. (John 3:16)

Now let's look again at the verse that follows this:

> For God did not send his Son into the world to condemn the world, but to save the world through him. (John 3:17)

John 3:16 seems to say what many religions teach: believe in Jesus in order to be saved. John 3:17 says Jesus came to save the world. There seems to be a contradiction here between what these verses say and what is commonly taught, which is that Jesus sacrificed himself in order to save the world. If you are told the work of Jesus cannot be completed until you choose to believe, doesn't that mean Jesus did not finish his job of saving the world?

The resolution has been to say that Jesus did his job and left you the choice to believe in him or not—you *might* be saved. Jesus is the Redeemer, but you must believe in him to be redeemed. Stop and think about whether these two ideas make sense together (Jesus saved the world; you must believe). If you feel confused, it can be tempting to just accept what you've been told to believe and not think about it too much. But wouldn't you agree that God does not want you to settle for confusion? God wants your clarity and understanding.

The only way to truly resolve the contradiction between these two ideas is to understand that you are already saved. With this understanding, you don't have to believe in order for salvation to happen. Rather, salvation has already happened and you believe in it—if, that is, you believe Jesus did what he came here to do ("For I did not come to judge the world, but to save the world").

Why would you not believe that Jesus finished his work? Did he not say, "It is finished"?[1]

Saying the world is already saved is another way of saying the sins of the world were forgiven. It is another way of stating that the Savior Jesus Christ came into the world and died that humanity should have spiritual life. It's not that Jesus died to save you; he died for you to know that you are saved. He did not come to bring the light to you; he came to inform you that you are the light.

The completion of Jesus' mission does not depend on your believing in him. Your Lord would not be very powerful if he required your belief to empower him. Rather, he is empowered already, and you choose to believe it. You are already saved, and you choose to believe it.

You might then ask, "Why do I (or anyone) need to believe, if I am already saved?"

---

1 John 19:30.

Being already saved means that God is real, which, in turn, begs the question: "If God is real, why do you need to believe in God?"

You need to believe in God in order to know God. God is real, whether you believe in God or not, but you can live your entire life without ever finding God. Likewise, you need to believe in the Son in order to know the Son—to be alive in Spirit.

This does not mean that unless you believe, there is no salvation. Salvation does not go away. If you don't believe in God, does that mean God goes away? You are saved whether you believe it or not; you just might not be participating in a relationship with God. You can choose to live in light or darkness, but your soul is not at risk, ever, of being permanently cut off from God.

Perhaps you've felt that already being saved was not news to you because you were already saved when you accepted Jesus Christ as your Lord and Savior. But you may also have been taught that the saving comes only after you die, as you enter heaven. Holding this view deprives you of the desire for the spiritual wealth available to you while you're alive.

If "believe in me and get to heaven" were the only message Jesus came here to deliver, the Gospels would have been four very short books. Do you not think God knew what he was doing? Do you think the Gospels are just four hefty books of rhetoric and sayings that don't really matter enough for anyone to read? The divinity of Jesus is not to be slighted, but neither should the full range of his teachings.

There is a greater spiritual purpose to your being here than knowing God's name and where you will go when you die. Jesus invited you to believe in and seek God because he knew you would find God if you did. He knew from firsthand experience that you would find more knowledge of Spirit with each passing day—with each passing hour—commensurate to the energy and faith you put into your seeking.

What you find is yours to keep. The treasures of eternal salvation are gained through earthly seeking. Would you like to leave this earth with nothing more than you came with? Or would you like to leave with trunkfuls of treasure? Will you choose to be saved only after you die? Or will you be saved while you live?

Despite the great faith you have in God, you might be surprised to learn how much thought you put into keeping him at a distance. There is much more than religious faith surrounding the belief that you will be awarded salvation only when you die, there is purpose behind it, driven by the ego.

The Reconciliation of Ego and God

It can be frightening to face ideas that conflict with your beliefs. For most of your life, any questions pertaining to God and what to believe may have been answered by your religion, and the great mystery of God reduced to a matter that need not concern you while you are alive, because you have all the answers you need for this life.

Consciously or unconsciously, having those answers is a great comfort. To entertain new ideas that conflict with those answers threatens that sense of comfort. You will either accept the new ideas and brave the unknown or deny their validity. If you were raised to believe xyz or else go to hell, and then someone comes along and says, "Here is abc, instead of xyz," you're probably not going to accept it. You might believe this is a simple matter of rejecting the new ideas, but there is more to it than that.

Words are just words. Ideas are just ideas. They only have the meaning you give them. Therefore, if hearing new ideas causes you to feel angry, offended, or frustrated, something deep within you is generating those feelings. To suddenly question what you know or believe can cause you to be spiritually afraid. Not only is much of what you thought for a lifetime called into question, but in that moment it can feel as if you've lost God, which in turn may cause you to worry about your salvation—whether you are still in good standing with God.

Ideas like being already saved, or of it not mattering (in a soul-threatening way) whether or not God wrote every word in the Bible, or that you can possibly know God now may open new doors of knowledge, but they also may go against everything you've known to be true about God and your religion for all your life. Entertaining new ideas at this point simply isn't worth the risk or the pain. You could feel exposed, vulnerable, and alone in very foreign territory—why volunteer for that?

Do these symptoms sound familiar by now? What is the part of you that responds from and adheres to a paradigm of separation? It's your ego.

As a separate being, your ego is constantly trying to protect itself in the guise of protecting you. It needs you to continuously feel secure. As long as you don't have a reason to question yourself, your ego is in no danger of your probing deeper and possibly discovering you have an ego. When suddenly you feel insecure about something related to your beliefs, your ego must act quickly. It may have you think, *I'm uncomfortable; avoid this.* Or it can make you feel offended. Remember, your ego has a much easier time justifying your opposition by telling you there is something wrong with new ideas you're presented or with the person presenting them than it would if you were to go digging into the foundations of your beliefs.

Your ego has been allowed to exist in its solitude so long as you have the spiritual answers you've been given to provide you with comfort. The concept that God loves you and is waiting for you in the afterlife is one that allows you to be alone while still knowing that God is up there somewhere. The separateness you may feel is considered natural—the earthly state of your being. The acceptance of this state is the reconciliation between ego and God. It allows faith in God and the separate being to coexist in you. It allows a religion of separation.

Your ego allows you to accept Jesus Christ as your Savior so long as you also accept that you are apart from him. You can be with him after this life if you believe in him. Ego will let you bask in holy feeling, worship God, and be as religious as you want, so long as you remember your place. You can dance in the sunlight, but you are not one with the sun.

As long as union with God is believed impossible for this life, ego is safe in its separation. This is why ego will so strongly defend Jesus as the only Son of God—the unique and only being who could be one with the Father—something you could never be. Shrouded in piety, the work of ego is hidden from sight. If Jesus was the only Son of God, who are you—the illegitimate child of God?

The ego is a savvy trickster. For example, when you read the words, "You are already saved," perhaps you were a bit shocked, but you kept on reading. Now imagine someone who read those words and threw the book down in disgust. He might have scoffed and denied the words had any possible value. He got angry, believing the words were an assault on his sacred beliefs. Maybe the words seemed so heretical that he thought they came from the devil. At such times, the ego sits back and smiles at a job well done—its position as secure as ever.

Your ego will summon cyclones of anxiety in you rather than leave itself exposed. It may cause you to think that all the discomfort you feel is being caused by the words you are reading. It may tell you that God, Jesus, or the Bible is being attacked. Your ego may tell you that your faith is being attacked. It knows how to strike the deepest chords to rally your defenses.

The ego won't tell you what's really going on: That it's not God, Jesus, the Bible, or your faith being called into question here. *It is the ego that is being called into question.*

You may have been taught you can only be with God after death, but the truth is, you are with God now, and you could live in conscious union with him. What you cannot do is be separate from God and one with him at the same time. By accepting this truth, you are putting your ego at grave risk—you are telling your ego there is a possibility that separate being cannot be. And while you may not be consciously aware of what this means, your ego does know—its inevitable annihilation. Even if you know that few, if any, people could ever overcome their ego completely, your ego knows only the real threat and does everything in its power to protect itself.

Abandoning the notion that you need to be saved is not abandoning Jesus Christ. You are only abandoning the belief that you are separate from God. Don't allow the voice of ego (yours or anyone else's) to convincing you otherwise.

What all this means is that your ego is not real. It is a construct of your psyche. It seems real and can be difficult to discern because its construction began when you were too young to be aware. However, God and your spirit are real; your ego is not. Your ego is a manifestation of your belief that you are separate from God.

Referring to ego as a separate being is a way to help clarify what's going on inside you. Of course you're not crazy and you're not possessed; obviously the ego is a part of you. When we speak about the ego thinking, or as a being, we are talking about you. It's the part of you that thinks of yourself as separate not only from God but also from others, and is characteristically consumed with how you look to others so as not to draw negative attention to yourself, which would lead you to examine your self-identification as a being in isolation from others.

If you are unaware of how your ego functions, the older you get the more developed it will be, and the harder it will be for you to break free of what you've become accustomed to believing is true. Yet you can never be so old that breaking free is impossible. If you look deep enough inside you will see that ego is like a great plant growing in a Petri dish—it has no natural roots. You can trace your ego's thoughts down to the true original sin: the incorrect thought of your isolated self, which drives the incorrect ways you can think, speak, and act.

Ego has only your conscious mind to work with—to hijack and leverage against you so that any momentary insecurity you might feel about facing something unknown quickly grows into full-on fear. You know yourself better than your conscious mind is aware. You know that your ego does not define who you are; there is much more to you than that. This is why you are drawn to God. You are predisposed to God, which means you are predisposed to who you truly are—a spiritual being who is at home in God's Spirit and truth, and you will therefore recognize his words.

If you believe in God, you believe that the spirit is eternal; you have a soul. You know the body is the temporary home of that soul. The world is the home of the body. Your ego is as temporal as your life in the world.

Ego the Ally

Before we give the ego a rest here, some last words.

The ego is not all dismal stuff. As you walk your spiritual path, your ego will rise to challenge you in more ways than can be captured here—by hiding in thoughts too familiar to recognize as ego, and by looking for new ways to tempt you from the truth of your higher self. Once you are aware of how it works, however, you can make a game of catching the little devil at work. You can use ego-driven thoughts as a way to become conscious of what you don't want and clarify what you do want.

imple, someone cuts you off in traffic and you're
1 give them the finger. Upon reflection, you are
bothered that you could let yourself be so easily affected and
behave in such a way, and you feel bad how you treated them
and don't wish to be that kind of person. Or maybe you are
at a party or a show and find yourself not paying attention to
what's being said or happening in front of you because you're
concerned how you look to others. You realize being present
is more important to you.

Your ego has been your ally as well as your enemy. The
ego is your protector, for better or worse. You may recall from
our discussion in Chapter 4 that the world of separation begins
very early in life—such as on the school playground. Your
ego protects itself by making sure you do not stand out, but
this also helps you to fit into the world. You act "normal;"
you make friends. You develop a sense of safety and security,
which can serve you your whole life.

As an adult, you need money to pay for food, shelter, medicine, or anything else you need. Your ego helps you to stay
focused on these realities. It can be beneficial to believe you
are alone because you are then driven to be self-sufficient.

God is with you, but you have to drive the car. You can
have the faith of a saint, but take your hands off the wheel and
you will crash.

Your ego keeps you grounded. If your experience of
God were to become too intense, you might no longer fully
respect what is required of reality. You might become
delusional—believing that knowing God is enough—
and not pay attention to surviving or doing all you must
to succeed in the real world. This might work for a dedicated

236

monk but not for anyone who wants to live a balanced life in the ego-dominated world.

If, for example, you were to suppose that since God heals, and you know God, you need not take care of your body. You might then become sick. Your weakened ego would quickly remind you that belief in God, and being realized as one with God (such that no sickness could touch you), are not the same. Or you might be an avid seeker with a great deal of spiritual information but when someone says something that triggers you to lose your temper, you quickly come to realize how strong your ego is and that you still have work to do if being spiritually realized is your goal. Or perhaps you experience the stark wake-up call of a financial failure. A crushed ego can work wonders to motivate you.

We learn from self-experience. Most of the examples in this section are lessons I learned about my own ego, more often than not, the hard way.

To call the ego the enemy is to discredit the good that it does. Ego is too much a fact of your makeup to not be seen as part of God's plan. Further, to call it the enemy is to empower it against you, because you then view it as something outside your control. You have to accept that you have an ego in order to see it, just as the addict must acknowledge the addiction before a new reality can be forged. With this acknowledgment comes clarity and strength—the knowledge of where you don't want to be and where you do want to go.

Whether we call it spiritual development, fulfillment, or realization, our desire for a relationship with God has that loftiest of goals—salvation. At some point, we will need to cross a line of allegiance to Spirit; we will have to work toward transcendence of ego. We will have to accept God's promise of a kingdom to find. For what is salvation truly if not permanent residence in Spirit—union with God.

What if union with God, which you imagine you will experience in heaven, you can begin to experience on earth? Fixed on the afterlife in heaven, the road of seeking ends when you are presented with and believe in the Son, and you are told that's as far as you can or need to go. Fixed on God and living your fullest life, the road can begin with Jesus and his teachings, and extend beyond the horizon, as far as you want to go.

Salvation Is Now

As with some of the other terms we've discussed, there is a spiritual definition of the word "saved" that is more profound than literally being saved from going to a bad place after you die. The spiritual definition has to do with your life on the earth.

In chapter 6 we discussed John 15:5: "I am the vine, you are the branches. Those who abide in me and I in them bear much fruit, because apart from me you can do nothing." This means that you have spiritual life flowing through you so long as you are consciously connected to God—you are keeping God and his teachings in mind and acting accordingly.

To stay connected to God *is* salvation. Believing in Jesus saves you not just because you believe Jesus is divine but because you believe God is real and here for you now, as exemplified in Jesus Christ. By following his example of faith in God, and his teaching to seek God, you come to know that the divine is in you as well, and you can commune with God within yourself.

Doesn't the very notion that you should abide in God, in and of itself, fundamentally conflict with any religious idea that your place is to be separate from God? If you couldn't know God now—how could you possibly abide in him? Jesus' words guide you into an active relationship with God. He wants you to know God personally, in your mind, heart, and soul. Salvation is coming to know God now, not in theory for later.

To be saved means to liberate yourself from fear, from ego-domination, from limitation, from darkness, from anything holding you down and preventing you from soaring. Wings are not reserved for angels. Jesus said, "With your faith you can move mountains."[1] Are these mountains not on earth? He said, "Everything is possible for one who believes."[2] Do you think he meant possible only in heaven? These messages were not the abstract inspirational words of a gracious Messiah; they are part of the truth Jesus lived to let you know. You can live in the same reality of Spirit that Jesus lived in. But if all you do is look up and worship, imagining divinity is reserved for heaven, you could miss this glorious truth of your life.

Eternal life remains the core reward of belief systems in Jesus' name. You've been told that eternal salvation will come after this life. But if eternal life is guaranteed for the faithful and it is initiated by your faith now, why do you have to wait for it? Because most people define eternal as refer-

1 paraphrasing Matthew 17:20; Mark 11:23.
2 paraphrasing Mark 9:23.

ring to the afterlife? Okay, but during this waiting period until you die, what happens if someone's faith wavers?

Let's say someone believes in Jesus Christ and therefore receives eternal life. What happens if he then changes his mind and no longer believes? Does he still have eternal life? If it can be taken away, is it truly eternal? Can something be everlasting and at the same time stoppable?

What does the word eternal mean, anyway?

In most dictionaries, "eternal" means without beginning or end. When it is said that eternal life will be yours after you die (if you believe rightly), you know what is meant, but technically the idea doesn't make sense. Eternity does not begin at a fixed point in the future and extend forever; it has no beginning. It would be more correct to express that idea by saying you will be with God forever in heaven (if you believe rightly). This is why you will not find a single instance in the Bible telling you that eternal life will be yours after you die. The Bible says eternal life will be yours if you believe. It is a critical distinction.

I offer you that Jesus did not come to show you the way to eternal life later; he came to show you a state that exists now, eternally. It is the kingdom of God. It is the realm of Spirit—always present—like God's forgiveness—eternally true. How his heart yearned for you to see this truth.

> Do not be afraid, little flock, for it is your Father's
> good pleasure to give you the kingdom.
> (Luke 12:32)

Everyone who asks receives.

(Matthew 7:8; Luke 11:10)

Jesus brought you the gift of knowing that the kingdom is already here for you. What you believe in precedes your belief in it; it existed long before you got here.

This is not to say there is no kingdom called heaven for you to be in after you die. There has been no comment on that here; your beliefs are your own. Whatever any of us believes, no one knows for sure what happens when we die, much less the details of what the place we go to is like, but we *can* know of a kingdom on earth. If you do believe that you will still exist after this life, then you believe there is some heavenly part of you that transcends mortality.

Eternal life is not disconnected from this life. What is your soul but eternal life, housed for a time in your body? You connect with the Spirit of God inside you, within your soul. Ironically, it can be easier to accept a kingdom that exists only in the afterlife because there is then no reason to seek one now. The kingdom is so desired that many people allow the fate of their soul to depend on their faith in the future kingdom, yet they will ignore the possibility that the kingdom is also available to them right here.

Jesus shows you a path that requires discipline and perseverance—to stay righteous and never give up on seeking God—but the rewards are your entrance into the kingdom of heaven on earth. Is this too good to be true? You choose the answer according to your faith and seeking. As you are awake in your life, so shall you be in heaven. You don't need to wait

until you are dead to walk in the bliss of God. You don't have
to wait until you're dead to know God personally.

Now turn this understanding of eternal to the idea of
eternal punishment or eternal fire—terms that have scared
so many of us for so long, generation upon generation, age
after age. We haven't allowed for the possibility of eternal
life without eternal death.

Eternal life is the same thing as no death. In the Gospel
of John, Jesus indicates that to believe in him or his words is
to not be subject to death.

> For God so loved the world that he gave his one
> and only Son, that whoever believes in him shall
> not perish but have eternal life. (John 3:16)

> Very truly, I tell you, whoever keeps my word will
> never see death. (John 8:51)

Death is separation from God, so now we are talking
about eternal separation. Not keeping God and his words in
mind (which can also be called ignoring wisdom and good
sense) we are subject to living only according to our selves
and our actions. If we harm ourselves or others (sin), we suffer the result of those actions (death).

As we've discussed, this perceived state of separation, also, does not occur at some point in the future, but is experienced now. It has always been and will always be this way. And our suffering will be continuous if we don't change. We are fated to not improve or mature in our development because of our refusal to learn lessons, change our ways, or heed God's words. We repeat our mistakes, indefinitely, until we use our lives wisely to learn God's lessons. This self-inflicted punishment is everlasting until we stop the cycle of darkness.

If you believe that God is loving in nature, then believe that God's system of judgment is also part of a loving process. Wrath is an ancient-school way of thinking. The law of cause and effect is as much a natural part of our existence as the fact that if you roll a ball down a hill it won't stop before it reaches the bottom, unless it is impeded. If you have a fight with someone you love, and you say something you regret, the judgment you receive as a result is simply that the other person will be hurt and you will feel bad. Your salvation might be to apologize from the heart. Your condemnation might be some minor, everlasting suffering until you do.

If you cut yourself, you will bleed. This is the condemnation. Your salvation is learning to be more careful the next time.

The repercussions of our mistakes, weaknesses, sins, faults, and the opportunity they offer to learn and grow are all human affairs and part of the natural order of things. We take care of our own judgment just fine. If you can believe God created the world and left us free will, then perhaps he also left us a system by which we can either learn from our mistakes or ignore them, thus creating our own outcomes.

I ask you again, what would it possibly benefit God or you to have you burn in eternal hellfire? When will we cross the transformational line and be aghast that we have held onto these archaic beliefs for two millennia? We must allow ourselves to break free of this madness.

Jesus teaches you spirituality based on life, not death. He tells you to love and seek God, now. He teaches you how to perceive the kingdom, now. He tells you to be a good person now and to love everyone. He tells you to renounce sin—to stop choosing to be separate from God. No matter what you want to believe happens after you die, or at the end of the world, Jesus wants you to be fulfilled and to know God, now.

> He is God not of the dead, but of the living.
> (Mark 12:27; Matthew 23:32; Luke 20:38)

> Strive first for the kingdom of God and his
> righteousness ... do not worry about tomorrow,
> for tomorrow will bring worries of its own.
> Today's trouble is enough for today.
> (Matthew 6:33–34, abridged)

He tells you plainly not to worry about tomorrow. Doesn't that seem to contradict the notion that you should

be not simply worried but downright terrified of n_i
it into heaven when you die? He tells you to strive ₁ᵤ.
kingdom of God and righteousness in the same sentence. You
could not strive for righteousness if it were not an earthly
matter and it is same for the kingdom of God in this context.
And why would Jesus say to strive for the kingdom at all, if
you only needed to believe in him? It is in times like this—
when confusion and contradictions arise—that you are told,
"God's ways are not our own. He is beyond our understanding." God is beyond your understanding, but the words in the
Bible are there for no purpose other than your understanding.

Jesus' most important evangelist, Paul, beseeches you in
his letters to find the rewards of Spirit, which he says are here
for you now.

To set the mind on the flesh is death, but to set the
mind on Spirit is life and peace. (Romans 8:6)

God's love has been poured into our hearts
through the Holy Spirit that has been given to us.
(Romans 5:5)

The verse above says that God's love and Holy Spirit *have
already been given.* Do these messages lead you to focus your
attention on the rewards of death? Do they sound like they are
in any way intended to evoke fear? The time of your salvation
is now. Don't worry about eternity; eternity will bring worries
of its own. Today's trouble is enough for today.

Now is the time to move away from the fearful ancient belief that the only meaning for your life is to learn what you need for salvation after death. Now is the time to free yourself from the fear that ignores Jesus' full range and depth of spiritual teachings in favor of a single ultimatum to choose heaven or hell. Now is the time to free yourself to seek and find the kingdom that Jesus lived, labored, suffered, and died to present to you. To know the kingdom of Spirit is to know you are part of it. Don't reconcile yourself to remaining a separate being in a separate world—a purgatory on earth—until death brings your salvation. Choose the spiritual life that Jesus offered you, now.

Free yourself from ultimatums. Find the love first; learn what's right second. Jesus would rather you be happy than have the right answers. Jesus would rather you feel the love inside than even know his name. Perhaps the issue of what to believe should be put on hold until you can equate God with love and do not link fear to what you believe. Once you have arrived at that place, you can return to your beliefs with a new understanding that comes from within, not from something you were taught or commanded to believe.

CHAPTER 11

LIBERATION

John Restored

I am the way, and the truth, and the life. No
one comes to the Father except through me.
(John 14:6)

Whoever believes in him is not condemned, but
whoever does not believe stands condemned
already because he has not believed in the name
of God's one and only Son. (John 3:18)

Remember that in both these situations Jesus is talking as
the fully realized Son of God. He is the Christ. This is Christ
talking directly to you. It might be easier to understand this if
you remove the name Jesus from your thoughts for a moment.
Think of the Son of God here as pure Spirit. Spirit stands in
a body before you and says, "I am the way, and the truth, and

247

the life. No one comes to the Father except through me." Spirit stands before you and says, "Whoever believes in me is not condemned, but whoever does not believe is condemned already, because he has not believed in the Spirit on earth."

For so long, you have created a Jesus Christ as you imagined him to be based on all you've been taught and the perspective of your own life experience. A personality has been imprinted onto the name Jesus—the Lord, the Savior, the one and only Son of God—who is separate and removed from you. It is natural that the way you've seen Jesus is based on how you see yourself. Seen from your perspective, Jesus is removed from you because you see yourself as being removed from him.

You accepted the reconciliation: Jesus is up there and you are down here; he is the Savior and you a lowly sinner. The relationship is exactly as it should be, according to a belief system of separation. Jesus is the Son of God, after all, and you know you are not.

How Jesus labored and beckoned your soul to see who you truly are—how like him you are—beloved by God, with open-ended possibility for your relationship with God. In better recognition of who you are could you be ever inspired in your seeking to know God better. Jesus knew that the kingdom of God is in *you*. Jesus knew what people were not ready to hear:

Only through yourself can you know God.

Only through yourself can you know anything. Remember what we discussed back in Chapter 1 about learning to drive?

LIBERATION

You can't learn to drive by sitting in a classroom; you have to get behind the wheel and practice. Only through yourself—through your own experience of making mistakes and correcting them—do you become better. This is how everything is learned. Or, remember the difference between memorizing multiplication tables and understanding of the principle of multiplication? Two sticks laid out two times gives you four sticks.

Or consider someone with whom you fell deeply in love. Chances are, you did not feel that way the moment you met them. True, lasting love grows from intimate interaction and experience.

All this is also true about your relationship with God. You can believe in God with all your heart. You can love God with everything you are. But you can only grow in your understanding of God through your own experience of him. Wouldn't you like to know God, rather than just believe in or pray to him? Wouldn't you like to know God the way Jesus did when he lived?

Wouldn't you like to know for yourself which are the words of God and which are the words of men? Come to know spiritual truth through yourself and you will become an authority on the Bible.

Trust no other source but yourself to determine what is truth. Trusting an outside source is for those who have not trusted in their own capacity to understand the words of God. For spiritual matters, stay true to the source that defines you: your relationship with God. Walking your own path is the only way you can know anything. Come to know, rather than settle for belief.

If you keep on seeking, one day you are going to find that as you learn who you are you will learn for yourself who Jesus

249

Christ was/is. You will come to understand him and relate to him through your own spiritual knowledge, gained through your own spiritual experience. Your knowledge of Jesus, or God, will always be a perfect reflection of what you know of yourself. This is because:

There is no separation.

The only separation possible is the one you choose to imagine and believe in—you can stay fixed on the idea of it. God is here with you now. The kingdom is not a place you find; it is where you already live. If you stay true to the path of seeking and never give up on its course, you will arrive at the truth:

You are one with God.

Call it God, Christ, Allah, Spirit, Yahweh, or any of the other myriad names given to the higher power since the dawn of humanity—you're made from the same stuff. You may believe you can only be one with God when you die. You may believe only Jesus could be one with the Father while alive. You may believe that if you follow the path of seeking long enough, you could one day attain oneness with God. The truth is, you are one with God right now. You just may not be aware of it. You may not believe it, but you cannot be separate from God.

"No one comes to the Father except through me."
"me" is you.

"Whoever believes in the only Son of God is not condemned."

You are the Son of God.

Does this sound blasphemous to you—to call yourself the Son of God?

It is written that when Jesus was at a feast in Jerusalem, a mob surrounded him, saying, "If you are the Messiah, tell us plainly," to which Jesus replied, "The Father and I are one." The mob picked up stones to stone him, accusing him of blasphemy, that a mere man should claim to be God. Jesus answered, "Is it not written in your law, 'I said, you are gods'? If those to whom the word of God came were called 'gods,' can you say that the one whom the Father has sanctified and sent into the world is blaspheming because I said I am God's Son?"[1]

Jesus is referring to Psalm 82, in which God addresses a heavenly assembly he calls "gods," who later get condemned by God to be mortals. Jesus is basically saying to his accusers: if in your own law (the Old Testament) anyone other than God can be called gods, why shouldn't I be able to call myself that?

The tricky thing about spiritual words is that you interpret them according to your own spiritual understanding. When Jesus said, "I and the Father are one," he spoke his own truth.

1 John 10:22–36, abridged.

To others his truth seemed like blasphemy.

He spoke this truth because Jesus Christ was the fully realized spiritual being—the fully realized Son of God, unconstrained by ego. He was the expression of oneness with God; God in the flesh. There was no bushel basket over his flame; the light shone purely like the sun.

This light preached to you that you too could shine like this. You have the same light inside you, and Jesus wanted to bring it out of you— to set it on a hill for all the world to see[1]—as if to say, *Behold, I am. As I am, so too can you be.* The good news was for you. That you believe in Jesus as your Lord—that he was sanctified and sent into the world by God— should cause you to accept his message concerning your own capability and his wish for your realization. He spoke as you, for you, to show you who you are. To push him away in only worship is to deny his message.

The Son of God[2] is the god within you. It is your soul. It is your true identity. The Son of God is Christ within you. Your spiritual path is one of accepting your true, higher self (your Self). There is only one Son living through all of us, of which you are a part, and which is a part of God. Whoever sees the Son of God within themselves, sees who Jesus was, and Christ is.

---

1 "You are the light of the world. A city built on a hill cannot be hid." (Matthew 5:14).

2 Or the Daughter of God—same meaning. The Son is not a term of gender here but a term of universal spirit.

It might seem that to accept yourself as the Son of God is worse than blasphemy, because it sounds like you're claiming to be equal to Jesus Christ. Remember, however, that to acknowledge the divinity in yourself is not the same as declaring yourself a fully realized spiritual being. You are declaring that you are a spiritual being with the *potential* to be fully realized. By doing this, you are accepting one of the Gospel's main lessons.

It would indeed be blasphemous to state that you are the fully realized Christ in the flesh when you are not. Yet it would be equally blasphemous to state that you could never be.

The distinction between you and Jesus is one of realized potential. When you understand that, you turn the wall that separated you from God into an open door. It is the "open door, which no one is able to shut."[3] Even though Jesus promised that you could find the kingdom of God and know God, the egos of men denied it almost immediately after Jesus said the words. That denial was like another fall from grace, as it was when Adam and Eve fell.

Your own ego does not want you to accept your divinity. The ego wants you to accept your separation from Jesus Christ, who was unique among all human beings who ever lived or ever will live. Comfort in separation is the game of the ego. But you know better now. You are quickened with the words your soul can recognize.

As the fully realized living God, Jesus was love incarnate. As he lived, he could not help loving you and all his fellow human beings. Jesus acted as the great pioneer who found the Promised Land downriver and shouted back for you to follow.

3 Revelation 3:8.

He did not intend for you to know the Promised Land only after you died.

If Jesus meant that no one except him could know God, why does he teach you to seek God? He leads you to the truth that God has been with you all along, even though you may not have been consciously aware of it.

It is as correct for *you* to say, "No one can come to the Father, except through me." The only Spirit you can know is the one you are a part of (not apart from). Jesus' saying these words with reference to himself means that they are true for you as well, because he spoke as Spirit, as Christ, and Christ is within you.

> On that day you will know that I am in my Father,
> and you in me, and I in you. (John 14:20)

Your soul is in your body. God is found within you. You may have not yet spent enough time learning about spirit to fully understand the implications of the words "except through me," as Jesus did, but the same truth is waiting for you. The truth is always the truth. Many roads of seeking lead to this one master truth:

You are god.

This is another way to identify who you are—your spiritual Self; "god" is another way of saying Son of God. The life of Spirit on earth that dwells within each one of us is god; it is an identity we all have in common. You can cling to the delusion that you are separate as long as you choose; you can be a slave to your ego your entire life. Or, you can set yourself free by acknowledging the truth of your godly nature.

A few pages ago I cited Psalm 82:6, which Jesus quoted to those accusing him of blasphemy. In the full verse, God says to his heavenly assembly, "You are gods, children of the Most High, all of you." If you believe everything in the Bible was written on purpose, then it is no accident that Jesus cited this verse and used this vocabulary for you to relate to. If God can refer to any others beside himself as "gods," and if you believe God created you and blessed you by sending you into this world, should it be blasphemy for you to consider yourself the Son or Daughter of God?

Look to the words of both Jesus and Paul, as they apply this language to you. Jesus said, "Love your enemies, do good … and you will be children of the Most High."[1] This is whom Jesus beseeched you to become. It is part of the good news being delivered to you. Paul wrote, "For all who are led by the Spirit of God are children of God."[2]

Christ is the living God. Christ is not only within you, Christ is you. And Christ in all of us together is the kingdom, which is part of God's kingdom. These are not my words; they are Christ's words. Union is the truth, and separation has been the delusion.

1 Luke 6:35.
2 Romans 8:14.

You are a magnificent child of God for whom anything is possible. Now you can more intimately understand the words "No one knows the Father except the Son." Likewise, "no one knows the Son, except the Father" —only you can know God through yourself and no one knows you like God. If you relentlessly seek God, you will come to know him intimately, and you will know him more each day, which is to know yourself more, as well.

Once you overcome all your fears, relinquish all ideas of separation, embody love as a fully realized shining beacon of light in the world, and you live in perpetual, conscious union with God because he is living fully in the flesh through you, then you can say that you are [state your name] Christ.

Maybe you will not get there, but God's truth says you can.

The tables have turned. A new mob in Christ's name says, "Who are you, a mere person, to call yourself the Son of God?" In love you can answer, "I am who the Lord tells me I am." Or fear can prompt you to recoil from and reject everything you've been reading here.

You may think you are being humble when you say you are not the Son of God and worship the one who was. But, in truth, you are then not living up to the ideal Jesus said was possible for you. And so, in fact, you are saying you know better than God. You are saying you know better than Jesus.

You are saying, "I am *not* the light of the world." "I am not a child of God."

You don't want to be governed by your ego any longer, do you?

A lifetime of beliefs and practices—a way of thinking—does not come undone in a day, nor is it meant to. If you want to take a few seeking steps in a new direction, you will move at the speed that is best for you, and you will regularly find yourself in just the right place on your path.

None of us is perfect. Even Jesus Christ—the Son who walked in fully realized divinity—had his moments of doubt. Hours before his arrest, which he knew would lead to his crucifixion, he prayed: "My Father, if it is possible, let this cup pass from me."[1] And when he was on the cross, he cried out: "My God, my God, why have you forsaken me?"[2]

These words show the humanity of Jesus. They should bond you to him, and to the truth of your godliness even in your imperfection. Jesus did not intend for you to consider him different in nature from yourself. That he was the same as you (in being, soul, and living potential) is the salvation he presents you—it is your bridge to the kingdom of God.

Free your mind, heart, and soul. You are the living god. You can rest in humility and love, knowing that everyone else is god too. The only difference between one person and another is the degree to which each one has accepted who he or she is and realized his or her spirit in the world. You are the way, the truth, and the life, can you believe this?

---

1 Matthew 26:39; Mark 14:36; Luke 22:42; "Let this cup pass from me" is a metaphor—he doesn't want to drink the fate of suffering that is in the cup.
2 Mark 15:34; Matthew 27:46.

Will you listen to Jesus? He said:

> nor will they say, "Look, here it is!" or "There it
> is!" For, in fact, the kingdom of God is within you.
> (Luke 17:21)

Break free of what others tell you is the Gospel and hear it with your own ears. Read it with your own eyes. Recognize it through your own soul. Don't look outside yourself. Don't look anywhere else. The kingdom of God is found only within you.

Realize the god within you. Fighting your union with God is like a drop of water trying to separate itself from the rest of the ocean. But that is what most of us spend a lifetime doing.

Save yourself and you will be saved. You will be saved from ignoring the love God has for you and what God wants you to know. You will be saved from your own fear. You will be saved from your ego. If your life tends to be a living hell, you will be saved from hell.

You will rejoice in love. You will dance in happiness. You will glow in spiritual realization. You will speak the Word of God. You will live as your higher Self. You will know heaven on earth.

CHAPTER 12

EXALTATION

Do not fear fear anymore.

Joy joy!

The kingdom of God is at hand. It was in your midst all along.

You are the light of the world. Let your light shine in the world.

You are the doorway through which love enters the world. Dance and sing and leap for joy! For fear is no more. Fear has always been a choice. Fear has always been ignor-ance. Fear has always been ignoring what Christ tells you—not told you, for the word is living in the present.

The words above are pure in meaning. Do not allow them to be hijacked by religious interpretation.

Take fear out of the word Christ.

Christ is just a word of spiritual understanding, which refers to the Son of God.

Disempower words. Do not give them control
over you.

Words are just words. They have no spiritual meaning
beyond what you give them.

Take the stigma out of the word God.

If fear can't be removed from the word God, perhaps take
the word God out of your vocabulary. Try replacing it with
Love for a while and see how your experience changes.

Disempower your religion. Do not give it
control over you.

Religion is just religion. It is not God. Religion is there to
serve you; you are not here to serve religion.

If your religion serves your well-being it is a blessing.
Guiding your relationship with God, teaching you about Spirit,
love, seeking, and joining you with other likeminded believers
is religion's beautiful function fulfilled in your life. Religion
can also be a good reason to keep you part of a community.

However, if you are troubled by aspects of your religion,
or find contradictions between what you feel about God and
what you are being taught, take a break. Your religion won't go
anywhere. Don't be afraid to do what's right for you—that's
what's important. If you are afraid, it's a sign that something
is wrong. You are love incarnate; that's why fear feels wrong.
Nurturing the love within you is what matters most. Whatever
church, belief system, or practice you choose as a means to

serve your relationship with God, make sure the choice comes purely from you and not from fear of disobeying a choice that was made for you by others.

Disempower the Bible. Do not give it control over you.

The Bible is just a book—perhaps the greatest book ever written; perhaps not. The Bible is not the Gospel, though the Gospel resides there. Man's ego let in some bad news also—as a long-term tenant. The Bible is there to serve you; you are not here to serve the Bible.

You are the Son or Daughter of God, and so is everyone else.

Free yourself from the notion that there is only one way to find God or spiritual understanding.

There are many ways and places to learn in the world. There are books that will change the way you see everything, written thousands of years ago, hundreds of years ago, decades ago, last week. Open yourself up to learn from spiritual sources other than the Bible. Other perspectives can often help you to understand the same universal truths. Hindu spiritual texts might shed light on a sentence of Gospel that you never quite understood. Buddhism teaches you to free yourself from the suffering that results from a continuous cycle of darkness and ignorance, which is exactly what Jesus taught.[1] Literature from the natives of America might guide you to arrive at a deeper connection to the earth. Only the fear generated and used against you by your ego would deny you access to the whole of God's great library.

> Free yourself from what others tell you are the words of God or who they tell you God is.

Though many good teachers will teach you, do not take at face value any truth that is told to you. Remember blind faith as the face of the flower lying on the ground, which of itself will wither, versus the practicing faith of your personal seeking, which is the whole flower grown from the root. Believe only what you find through your own experience to be true.

> Practice freeing yourself from fear until you are.

Fear is not of God. Fear has never been anything but the servant of separation. To choose fear is to make a conscious choice to believe you are separate from God. It is to believe a lie. You cannot choose fear and love at the same time. To free yourself from fear, you don't need to fight fear. Choose love, and fear will evaporate. The great news is that love is the truth of who God is and who you are. To choose love is to choose the truth over a lie.

---

1 "If your eye is unhealthy, your whole body will be full of darkness. If then the light in you is darkness, how great is the darkness!" (Matthew 6:23)

God is Love. You are god. You are love itself.

The only hope of knowing God is to know yourself. Humbly submit to what you know and don't know at this time, even if that means you don't understand some of the things Jesus said, or don't fully understand who he was, or have doubts about any of the stories you've been told, or if you have any questions at all. As you seek them, the answers will come.

To understand Spirit is to know that you grow in Spirit constantly. Depending on your passion for seeking, you can grow one spiritual day over the course of a whole life, or you can grow a whole spiritual life every day. Who you were yesterday is not who you will be today, and you will be new again tomorrow.

Remember the tree we discussed back in Chapter 1 whose trunk stays true to the roots but whose branches extend and leaf each season? Being reborn is not a one-time thing. It happens many times over the course of your spiritual life. It can happen every day. You simply need to be open to letting Spirit show you who you are now. There is more to find on earth than you dream of there being in heaven. If you have faith not just in God but in the understanding that you can know God now, you will come to know God now. This is not some fluffy inspirational talk. This is the plain truth. These are facts.

I have told you I am within you. I have told you
to seek me for yourself. Jesus told you this.
Faith in God and faith in yourself are one and
the same. I made you to find me; believe it.
Don't display me your great faith by believing
in me. Show me your faith by finding me.

If you have this faith, you will find me, and
you will know me. If you do not have this faith,
you will not know me, and you will only be
able to believe in me and make what other
assumptions you will. A separate being thinks
in separate ways.

I am you; you are me; know that we are
one. The time is now. I am at hand. This is the
Good News.

Free the name Jesus from religion.

This does not mean removing Jesus from religion. This does
not say a religion created in Jesus' name can't serve you well. It
means Jesus and religion should not be inextricably linked. Jesus
created no religion. Religions were built in his name after his
death. It is important not to lose sight of this reality so that the
manmade institutions do not then become labeled as God-made,
and religious principles do not become labeled principles of God.
These religions serve Jesus' purpose; they do not chaperone him
to you. God is sacred. The religions created in his name are not.

This is not a call to abandon religion. This is not a denunciation of religion. It's a reminder that religion is not supposed to have power over you. Religion is there to serve God by serving your relationship with God, and this warrants reverence. But only man's ego ever took his religion too seriously—using your faith in God as leverage to have you conform to his religious constructs and beliefs.

A religion created in Jesus' name is ideally an organization of people who share the same beliefs, gathering together in worship and love to share and explain his messages, and to learn and grow together. That gathering should be without pretension—no fear, no sanctimony, no dreary services, no ultimatums, no threats, no judging others, no condemning others, no believing there's nothing more to learn. The love of God should be as pure as the laughter of a three-year-old being tickled.

Jesus would rather you were happy and loving God than worried about his being the Lord. Jesus would rather you seek for yourself than be told the answers. Jesus would rather you love your fellow human beings and not believe in him, than worship him daily and not love your fellow human beings.

AFTERWORD

The Gospels are four dense books, yet perhaps we can summarize the messages of Jesus according to his two highest commandments: love God and love others. If each one of us did no more than love others in our hearts and in practice, we would have peace on earth. The message of Jesus was simple. Man's ego made it complicated. *New Words* has focused mostly on his first commandment: love God.

To love God is to seek God. When you are in a relationship with a person you love, if you did nothing more than simply worship that person, the relationship would not last. You work at it. With determination and commitment, you expend the energy to make the relationship work. The same holds true for your relationship with God. You declare your love for God by seeking God daily. This doesn't have to be a rigorous, ascetic struggle. It can be simply a desire, intention, and some time used daily for that seeking.

For all the great value of congregation with others, you must put in the time to be alone with God. You could be reading, meditating, strolling in a park and letting your thoughts unwind, or just sitting up in your bed at night. But you have to make the time. Why? Because the rewards are worth it. Being consciously in tune with God seems enticing, doesn't it—actually perceiving that God is with you, hearing God's guidance, thinking higher thoughts, speaking and acting in a wiser manner, living a life governed by love?

Having accepted Jesus' instruction that you should seek, how exactly do you do that? It seems only sensible that you first have to believe in a God/Spirit present here and now for you to know. The surest way to then seek God/Spirit is through meditation. I can only say this based on my own experience, as well as relay the counsel of every spiritual teacher I respect and have learned from. I believe this is what Jesus referred to when he said, "When you pray, go into your room, close the door and pray to your Father, who is unseen."[1] The privacy of your own consciousness is where you commune with God, so while I've certainly had plenty of revelations outside or in public—sometimes at the least expected times or places—meditation takes place in a controlled environment, ideally quiet, with no distractions, where you can travel inward, deeper and deeper into that meditative state. Therefore, meditation is the most efficient way to facilitate communion with God.

"Meditate" (in order to know God, or to find peace and clarity) is something you may have heard preached and prescribed so many times throughout your life that it sounds like a cliché. But sometimes clichés are the simple result of the truth always being the truth. This is one truth repeated

---

1 Matthew 6:6, abridged.

by all prophets and sages since time immemorial that you don't want to ignore.[2]

Many of us don't try to meditate because it sounds intimidating. Instead of setting unrealistic goals such as, "Starting tomorrow I'm going to meditate every morning and night for an hour," say that you will commit to meditating every day for some length of time, even if it is no more than five to ten minutes. You can gradually increase the amount of time—even if it is by just one minute each week. It's not necessary to keep track of time, but it can be helpful in the beginning as you get used to the process. There are no rules about how much time you should spend at each sitting, but making the time daily is key.

Meditating can be difficult at first if you're not used to quieting your mind, but you get used to it fairly soon and the rewards come quickly. It's a pretty simple process: have on loose-fitting clothes (if possible; not required), sit comfortably on the floor or in a chair with your back and neck straight, close your eyes, and just be—open and receptive. You want to practice the art of not thinking; as rambling thoughts may come, let them go. I will usually start by asking God to please come through to me, to guide me and my life to be in service to us all, to let my thoughts be his, and then I sit receptively and in patience. You might say a prayer to Jesus, or have another understanding of God; the language is not important. What matters is quieting your thoughts, letting go, and staying open to receive. One who doesn't believe in God one can just as well sit and allow

---

2 If you want more instruction in meditation, you can easily find abundant material on the subject in books, on audio, online, or there are even a plethora of cell phone apps now.

clarity or wisdom to come. If you can only sit there for five to ten minutes in the morning, at least you will have the experience of sitting still each day. Even that short amount of time can alter the trajectory of your day for the better, and the days can change your life.

Perhaps you will gain some insight into a problem you were having. Or maybe you will simply feel refreshed. Sooner rather than later you may find yourself wanting to spend more time in that state. One day you will have your moment of connecting with something greater than yourself. Once you experience yourself knowing more—perceiving God more—and evolving as a spiritual being, you'll get hooked. Meditation helps every area in your life because it helps you, who are the center of everything you do. Remember the ultimate reward you're promised for seeking: nothing less than finding God.

I have found that the requisite complement to seeking is having love as your fundamental disposition and intention. You cannot get far in your seeking without it. This is the perfection of God's system. Seeking without love will find something, as all seeking does, but will miss the meaning—the feeling—the deepest fulfillment. Seeking without love is like listening to a recording of an orchestra as opposed to hearing one perform live.

When you give in to love, any ordinary moment can blossom into something extraordinary, and you with it. In whatever you are doing, you can consciously raise your awareness. You can think and feel with love and work it into any moment—into a conversation you are having with someone (by paying attention to what they are saying; appreciating them), into your meditations and thoughts about God or Spirit (feeling your desire to have God flood through you and guide you), into the experience of the nature around you (breathing in the air; seeing, hearing, and appreciating your surroundings), looking at your reflection in the mirror and loving yourself—you name it. As you choose love, your perceptions and feelings expand exponentially, the way a gray day transforms as the sun clears the passing clouds.

If it is not your normal practice, next time you hear a song you like, instead of just listening to it in the background, close your eyes and give yourself over to it fully. You will hear it open up to new depths in every direction, and you will feel great joy. When it is done you will have raised the vibration of your being.

You can learn a great deal about the realm of Spirit with just your mind, but love opens it up. Love is the key to the kingdom of heaven. You can try to deny this. You can also try to jump high enough to defy gravity. You are a being of love, and learning to live according to this truth is to find peace and harmony with who you are.

Jesus wanted you to know God—not just as some far off, incomprehensible supreme being to whom you pray, but as someone with whom you can actually communicate. If you seek God, he will make himself known to you in a way that only you will know. It will be a custom-tailored communication. Perhaps you will receive what seems like an intuition of spiritual understanding, maybe there will be some kind of wink of coincidence, or maybe you'll find yourself hearing just the right words at the right time. You will be amazed. *How is it possible that there are more than seven billion people on this planet and yet God has heard and spoken to me? How can God be guiding me and also all the other people as well?*

While none of us may ever comprehend how this happens, it is nonetheless true and can be experienced by anyone who chooses to seek God and never gives up. Faith that God exists is a good starting point, but faith that you can know God, followed by intention and the action of seeking, is a faith to which God responds.

The path begins with this kind of faith.

Believing in a future kingdom of heaven you'll be in after you die has its place and is your choice, but this belief should not be at the expense of the kingdom of Spirit present for you to know now. If you are still unsure of this eternal present, I believe that if you now keep on reading the Gospels for yourself, all the way through each one, you will find this to be one of Jesus' most prominent and repeated messages.

And if you can wake up while you're alive to the perspective of heaven on earth, and you can appreciate the grand wonder and beauty of this life, feeling how special this whole existence is, you will shed the tears of shivering awe and joy. You will be filled with a love that is overwhelming beyond words and expression. You will love who you are and you will know that loving every person is the only way to be in perfect harmony with God.

If you suffer, or live in spiritual bondage, I hope you will break free and break through. All the power is within you. By whatever name you call it, the great Spirit is with you, guiding you, blessing you, and loving you. You are the joy of the world.

Stop and smell a lily each day.

NEW WORDS

There are no new words really.
Matter of fact they're all old.

32351588R00171

Made in the USA
San Bernardino, CA
13 April 2019